Using Statistics

STOCK

to Predict and Optimize

MARKET

Investment Outcomes

PROBABILITY

JOSEPH E. MURPHY, JR.

PROBUS PUBLISHING COMPANY
Chicago, Illinois
Cambridge, England

ISBN 1-55738-564-5

Printed in the United States of America

BB

RR/BJS

1 2 3 4 5 6 7 8 9 0

Probus books are available at quantity discounts when purchased for business, educational, or sales promotional use. For more information, please call the Director, Corporate/Institutional Sales at (800) 998-4644, or write:

Director, Corporate/Institutional Sales
Probus Publishing Company
1925 N. Clybourn Avenue
Chicago, IL 60614
PHONE (800) 998-4644   FAX (312) 868-6250

To Diana, Michael, and John

Table of Contents

Preface

Although I have spent substantially all of my working life in the investment business, it took many years to develop the ideas contained here. I began my work in investments at a brokerage firm in Minneapolis, where I did research on common stocks. After several years at that firm, I was invited to join the trust investment department of Norwest Bank because of work I had done in applying the computer to investment research, an endeavor that, at the time, was relatively new.

As I did my apprentice work in the business, I learned and applied various techniques for choosing which stocks to purchase and which to sell. One commonly used technique was to project future growth of earnings based on past growth. Another was to project future growth based on certain ratios, such as return on equity. The theory or presumption behind these techniques was that high past return companies and companies with high rates of return on equity would show the greatest future growth of earnings and, therefore, also stock prices.

Because I wanted to be sure my stock selections were based on a solid foundation, I began to look for studies that would affirm the usefulness of the techniques I was applying. I quickly discovered that few such studies existed. Since there weren't many, I started to do my own investigation. I began to look at the question of randomness in corporate earnings, in the belief that earnings were a critical element in determining the behavior of stock prices. I wrote several articles that showed that the data did not support many prevailing views on the subject. I did a concluding paper on this subject with Russell Nelson, then a member of the finance department of the University of Minnesota and subsequently chancellor of the University of Colorado at Boulder and then president of Arizona State. We presented a paper at the Western Association about which the discussant, who fully understood what we had done, replied: "If what Murphy and Nelson say is true, then all of the modern theory of finance is false. Obviously, the modern theory of finance is not false." Our results, however, were fully supported by the data. We showed that it was erroneous simply to run straight lines through what was clearly random data, even though that's exactly what many people in the field were doing. Our results implied that some parts of current theories of finance were open to question.

Of great help and interest to me was Norwest's membership in the Institute for Quantitative Research, an organization funded by 30 organizations in the investment business, including leading banks, insurance companies, industrial corporations, and brokerage firms. I represented Norwest Bank at many of the institute meetings. Some of the early researchers who gave papers at the institute included Bill Sharpe and other academic students of the investment market.

In the course of listening to presentations at the institute and doing my own research, I discovered that most of the prevailing techniques had little predictive value. They could not be used to select stocks that would outperform the market. Not only that, but the theories proposed by some leading academics and others did not work very well in practice. Many of us who attended the institute meetings and worked in day-to-day investments felt that we were not learning things we could put to practical use. It seemed to me the key reason that many techniques did not work very well was that they were based on the incorrect assumption that linear relationships existed between stock prices and other variables that could be exploited for profit.

In an effort to derive better forecasting techniques, I began to look for an alternative way of looking at investments. In this, I was heavily influenced by an article by M. F. M. Osborne entitled "Brownian Motion in the Stock Market," which had appeared in the *Journal of Operations Research* in the late 1950s and had been subsequently reprinted in the then controversial book of readings called *The Random Character of Stock Prices*.

I was so impressed by Osborne's article that I suggested that he speak at one of the institute's semiannual meetings, which he agreed to do. I recall vividly a debate between Osborne and a leading researcher. The researcher had run regression equations through stock price data. Osborne had objected to the procedure, saying, as I recall, "You can't treat that kind of data that way." The two were looking at investment data from entirely different perspectives, and I was certain that only Osborne's perspective was useful.

A few years later, I asked Osborne to collaborate in looking at interest rates in a way that would derive probabilities of how interest rates changed. That collaboration led to a paper we gave at the Chicago Board of Trade semiannual seminar entitled "Brownian Motion in the Bond Market," and to my two books on how to use the results, *With Interest: How to Profit from Fluctuations in Interest Rates* and *The Random Character of Interest Rates*. In addition to working on interest rates, Osborne and I worked on a number of investment problems over the course of two decades.

One of these problems was how to predict the probability of corporate profit or loss as a way to distinguish good credits from bad. Osborne and I developed a technique for predicting the probabilities for individual companies based on current cash flow as divided by the standard deviation of past changes in cash flow. From this, we derived an estimate of the probability of future profit or loss. The probabilities and credit ratings were published and proved to be very accurate. The forecasts of probabilities differ from forecasts of specific events, such as those derived from regression and related techniques. I felt that the techniques we used could be applied to a number of other investment questions, including forecasting probabilities of stock price changes, earnings changes, and yield changes.

This book is concerned, in large part, with how those techniques can be used in other applications and provides examples of how to do so. The book also contains chapters describing Osborne's model, together with an example; why the stock market increases over the long run; how portfolios become undiversified over time; the importance of dividends to total return; and simple rules of what kinds of analytical approaches cannot be used to make predictions because of the underlying nature of stock market and other financial data.

This book is not like most other books on investments, primarily because it was conceived and written from a different perspective than most others. The basic premise of this book is that first differences in the natural logarithms of stock prices (and other financial variables) are random and form an approximately normal distribution. Further, the expected mean change in the natural logarithms (logs) of prices is zero and has a standard deviation (a measure of spread) that increases with the square root of time.

These concepts are not uncommon: every options trader assumes them, and they form the basis of the famous Black Scholes options pricing model. They have important implications—some of which conflict with important aspects of current investment theory, others of which have not been exploited as they might be. These other implications can be used to make predictions about the future, predictions that are relevant to deciding how and when to invest. The derivation and description of those implications forms the core of this book.

What is different about this book is that it takes the distribution of changes in stock prices (and other financial variables) and derives ways of making probability predictions. Such predictions include, for instance:

- Giving the probability of a price, or a company's earnings or revenues, being above or below a certain level at a particular future date.

- Estimating the various proportions individual stocks in a portfolio will have after various intervals of time following an initial equal investment in each stock.

- Making probability assertions about whether a company will suffer a loss next year or five years from now, based on any one of several ratios, such as return on assets, or profit margins.

- Estimating whether a dividend will be raised or cut.

- Giving the probability that interest rates will rise or fall a given percent.

- Knowing whether a ratio, such as return on equity, is useful in predicting future growth of earnings.

- Explaining why a stock or a portfolio of stocks, such as the Dow Jones Industrial Average or the Standard & Poor's 500, has a long-term growth and how to calculate the rate of growth from the lognormal distribution.

Other kinds of predictions made in this book are illustrated by the list of topics in the Table of Contents.

Textbooks and practical books on stock investments often talk about randomness in stock prices and the normal distribution but don't normally take the approach described earlier. Although some books deal with one or two of the topics covered here, they generally approach the subject from a different point of view. Their perspective is often what might be called linear; it is analogous to the perspective of Newtonian physics in which one attempts to fit a straight or curved line to the data.

Unfortunately, you can't fit straight lines to random data. Much of physical data is random and has to be treated in probabilistic terms, which led to Quantum theories of physics. In a linear world, you estimate specific quantities and forecast precise numbers. In a probabilistic world, a random world, you forecast only probabilities (as in gambling), not specific quantities. The realization of this has greatly increased, as suggested by the growing interest in nonlinear systems and chaos.

Seven new chapters have been added to this revised edition. They cover the probability of stock price changes for use in evaluating options, the probability of yield changes for various maturities and time periods for help in bond investment, rescaled range analysis (a technique recently applied to the stock market), the importance of the dividend to total returns, an alternate method of computing the standard deviation (from the high/low range) and an analysis of the beta coefficient. New material has been added to Chapter 6, together with an example of the market model. Chapter 15 has been expanded to include estimates of market returns from a new series of data. Chapter 17 has been revised with corrections and extensions of the underlying data. A new appendix has been added for use with options, which gives the probability of stock price changes for periods of three months or less. All of the tables have been brought up to date with data through 1991 or 1992.

Preface to the First Edition

This book describes new techniques that may be used to estimate probabilities of future events that bear on the investment decisions of an individual, a pension fund, or a corporation. Some of these techniques can be applied to investment in stocks, others to mutual funds, still others to bonds, or to a corporation's allocation of resources.

While the precise future of any investment cannot be predicted, it is possible to estimate probabilities of what is likely to happen. It is possible, for example, to estimate the probabilities of alternative returns on stocks, of changes in interest rates, or of the direction of corporate earnings and dividends. By estimating these probabilities, it is possible to refine the investment decision process, avoid choices that have a low probability of favorable outcome, and thereby improve investment returns.

Although the techniques described here are based on statistical methodology that is well established, many of the specific applications to investments are unique and have not been described elsewhere. The reason they have not been used elsewhere is that the perspective on which they are based is an uncommon one that differs from what is traditionally taught in business schools and practiced on Wall Street.

The techniques described in this book may be used in aiding investment decisions on your own portfolio, those of your customers, or those of your corporation. The techniques can help you better manage investment risk and should improve your investment returns. They may also give you a new perspective on the stock market and the fascinating world of investments.

Acknowledgments

The foundation for my understanding of the stock market came from Maury Osborne with whom I've been privileged to work for nearly two decades. The model of the stock market given in Chapter 6 is based on the model he described in his classic paper, "Brownian Motion in the Stock Market." Many of the other techniques described here came from my collaboration with him on various investment questions. Any errors contained in this book, of course, are mine alone.

I am also indebted to Sue Freese and Marlin Bree, for editorial suggestions and assistance, and to Jim Harris, Dick Schall, and Dennis Senneseth, for reading the original manuscript and making suggestions and corrections. J. Michael Jeffers of Probus helped me restructure the book.

Joseph E. Murphy
2116 West Lake of the Isles Parkway
Minneapolis, MN 55405

CHAPTER 1

Overview

Stock prices and corporate financial variables have certain fundamental characteristics that can be used to derive estimates of the future. These estimates, in turn, can be applied to evaluate investment decisions and to help set corporate financial policy. The fundamental characteristics of stock prices and financial variables therefore constitutes the basis for determining what kinds of statements can and cannot be made about the future.

The most fundamental feature of stock prices, corporate sales, and earnings is that these variables bear a very close resemblance to a *random walk*—typified by a drunk, wandering over a plain. It follows then, that first differences in the natural logarithms of these variables approximate a random series. While a random walk would seem to defy making any estimates about the future, it nevertheless has two major characteristics that are extremely important and useful:

1. A random variable (like first differences in the logs of stock prices) conforms to an approximately normal distribution. As the most common distribution in the world, the normal distribution is well-known and has been studied extensively. We can use that knowledge about the normal distribution to estimate the probability of future occurrences. The application of the normal distribution gives us an approximate and very powerful tool for making estimates about the probabilities of future changes in stock prices and in other financial variables.

2. The dispersion of a random variable, measured by the standard deviation, rises with the square root of the holding period, or time.

This square-root-of-time rule is true of differences in the logs of stock prices, earnings, and other financial variables. The rule applies both to the dispersion of a single series, such as the price of Microsoft and to the cross-section dispersion, or the dispersion across stocks. *Cross-section dispersion* is like the dispersion of particles of smoke emerging from a chimney. The particles gradually spread out in the sky.

We can use the second characteristic, the square-root-of-time rule, to estimate probabilities over time intervals of different lengths. By measuring the standard deviation of the series we are interested in and then combining the normal distribution and the square-root-of-time rule, we can make probability estimates about the future.

Such estimates can be made of the probable range of future values of such variables as returns on a single stock, returns on mutual funds, future earnings and dividends, and the probability of loss. The estimates are probability statements such as the following: the probability of a 20 percent return on this stock is only 1 in 20, or the probability of a 30 percent decline in earnings is 1 in 40. We can prepare a distribution of various outcomes and their probabilities.

Chapters 10 through 14 are devoted to showing how to make and use probability estimates.

Characteristics of Randomness

The lognormal distribution and the rise in cross-section dispersion over time have two additional characteristics:

1.   There is an upward bias to the average return on a portfolio of stocks whose individual returns form a lognormal distribution. The market will have a positive return, which can be computed from the standard deviation. Although this important feature was pointed out many years ago, it has been entirely neglected.

2.   For any equally weighted portfolio, we can estimate the future distribution of assets after any holding period. The same estimate can be made for the rankings of companies by sales, profits, or market values.

These two characteristics of randomness and the lognormal distribution—the positive return of the market and the terminal distribution—give us an overview of what is taking place in the stock market and the corporate world. It tells us what will happen to our stock portfolio if we do not change it and what our industry will likely look like after the passage of time.

These topics are covered in Chapters 15 through 17.

Other topics, which are related to the distribution of changes in stock prices, are covered in Chapters 18–25. Chapter 26 covers estimating the probability of various changes in bond yields.

Rules of Probability

Just as the stock market may be a form of betting on the future, the behavior of market prices, earnings, revenues, and other financial variables exhibit some features of a horse race. At the start of the race, all the horses are even. Halfway down the track, one or more horses take the lead, and a larger group lags behind. As the race continues, the spread between the horses, the dispersion, widens. At midpoint, the probability that the last horse will pass the first is low, yet the probability that the last will begin to catch up may be even.

Exactly the same things happen in the stock market. The largest company is likely to remain the largest; the company with the biggest share of market is likely to retain it; and the company with the highest return on equity is likely to continue to earn the highest return.

But if changes in the logs of stock prices and corporate earnings are approximately random, as they appear to be, then relative growth in one period will not bear any systematic relationship to relative growth in another. Size, share of market, return on equity, and past performance are likely to bear little relation to future growth. That means that last year's best mutual fund or stock will have only an even chance of doing better than average next year.

The above relationships may be derived from the underlying characteristics of random processes, such as stock price changes, and stated in terms of rules or laws. The rules suggest that it is very difficult to make a precise prediction, though it is quite possible to make a probability estimate. The rules also suggest that many common practices and beliefs are without merit.

Chapter 27 describes the rules, or laws, and how to apply them.

CHAPTER 2

The Standard Deviation, the Normal Distribution, and Natural Logarithms— Concepts Useful for Studying the Stock Market

To describe the stock market, we need concepts that adequately describe uncertainty, indeterminacy, and the behavior of highly variable data. We will use three such concepts throughout this book: the *standard deviation,* the *normal distribution,* and *natural logarithms.* To lay the groundwork for later discussion, each of these concepts will be defined thoroughly in this chapter. (Readers who are familiar with these concepts should proceed to the next chapter.)

The first two concepts—the standard deviation and normal distribution—are useful in describing indeterminate, highly variable data. Natural logarithms are used to homogenize data covering long periods in calculating the standard deviation and preparing tables of distributions. Let's consider each concept in turn.

The Standard Deviation

The *standard deviation* is a measure of the spread, or dispersion, of a set of numbers. It is defined as the square root of the variance, with the variance defined as follows:

$$\text{Variance} = \text{Sum} \, (\, \text{Value} - \text{Average Value} \,)^2 \, / \, (\, \text{Number of Values} - 1 \,)$$

The *variance* is the sum of the squares of deviations from the mean, as defined above. Since the square root of a number is always positive, the variance will always be positive, as well, even though many of the original numbers may be negative.

The standard deviation is the square root of the variance, and is defined as:

$$\text{Standard Deviation} = \text{Variance}^{0.5}$$

We can compute the standard deviation of annual returns on the Standard & Poor's (S&P) 500 stock index, shown in Table 2.1.

As you can see, returns on the Standard & Poor's 500 vary from year to year. The mean annual return was 14.6 percent and the standard deviation was 13.2 percent. In a normal distribution, two-thirds of the returns will fall within one standard deviation of the mean. The range of one standard deviation of the mean for the above data is from 1.4 percent to 27.8 percent. Six of the 10 returns in Table 2.1 do fall within one standard deviation of the mean value.

Table 2.1   Computation of Standard Deviation

Year	Annual Return	Annual Return Minus Avg. (14.6)	Column 3 Squared
	%	%	%
1981	-4.9	-19.5	380.2
1982	21.4	6.8	46.2
1983	22.5	7.9	62.4
1984	6.3	-8.3	68.9
1985	32.2	17.6	309.8
1986	18.5	3.9	15.2
1987	5.2	-9.4	88.4
1988	16.8	2.2	4.8
1989	31.4	16.8	282.2
1990	-3.2	17.8	316.8

Average return	14.6%
Sum of squared deviations	1574.9
Average of sum of squared deviations gives variance (1574.9/9)	175.0
Square root of variance gives standard deviation (175.0)	13.2%

The Normal Distribution

A *distribution* shows how many items are within each range of values. Examples are the distribution of stock prices and the distribution of yields on stocks. At any given time, so many stocks will have a yield of 1 to 1.9 percent, so many with a yield of 2 to 2.9 percent, and so on. A table giving the number of stocks in each yield range is called a *frequency distribution*. A frequency distribution is used to classify the values in an easy, shorthand way.

A *normal distribution* is, by definition, bell-shaped and symmetrical. The height and width of its curve is determined by the standard deviation. Normally, if the standard deviation is small, the distribution will be tall and thin; if the standard deviation is large, the distribution will be short and wide.

Both kinds distributions are termed *normal distributions*. For all normal distributions (again, by definition), 68 percent of the values lie within one standard deviation of the mean, and 95 percent of the values lie within two standard deviations of the mean.

If we know the standard deviation, we can state precisely what proportion of the values lie above or below the standard deviation from the mean or, even more useful, within any fraction or multiple of that standard deviation. Figure 2.1 shows a normal distribution and Figure 2.2 shows a lognormal distribution. First differences in the natural logarithms of stock prices will approximate a normal distribution (Figure 2.1), whereas first differences in the prices (as distinct from first differences in the *logs* of prices) will approximate a lognormal distribution (Figure 2.2).

The area of each curve in Figures 2.1 and 2.2 represents the proportion of values that lie within it. As we can see in Figure 2.1, two-thirds of the area lies within one standard

---

Figure 2.1   A Normal Distribution

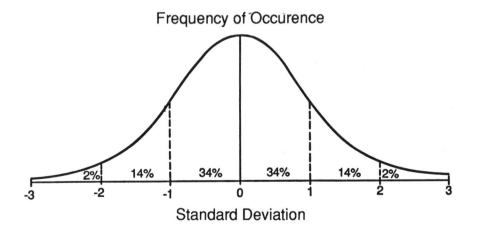

Figure 2.2   A Lognormal Distribution

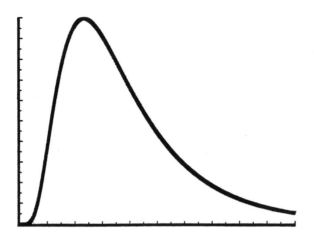

deviation of the mean, and 95 percent of the area lies within two standard deviations of the mean. Using a table for the normal distribution, we can calculate the proportion of values that fall within any range of standard deviations.

Stock returns, as defined below, conform approximately to a normal distribution. The distribution is not exactly normal because there are more large and small changes than there should be for a strictly normal distribution. As a result, the curve generated by stock price changes has a girth that is too narrow and tails that are too wide. Even so, the distribution is approximately normal.

Since the distribution is approximately normal, we can determine the distribution of historical stock returns over a given period, compute the standard deviation of that distribution, and fit that distribution to the normal curve. The normal distribution can then be applied to estimating the probability distribution of future stock returns. By doing so, we will have used the normal distribution as a model of what has taken place in the past and of what is likely to take place in the future.

Natural Logarithms

The degree of change in a stock price series tends to be proportional to the price level of the series. That being the case, dollar changes in stock prices are highly dependent on the price levels of the individual stocks, or the stock market index, whichever we are using. If we express the prices in terms of their natural logarithms, on the other hand, we obtain a new series in which variation in the series will not be dependent on the price level. The series will be homogenized, so to speak, like an egg after it has been beaten. All references to logarithms in this book are to natural logarithms, or to $\log_e$ (not to common logarithms; i.e., not to logarithms to the base 10).

Natural logarithms are useful for computing rates of return using continuous compounding. For returns of from 1 percent to 15 percent, the log change is close to the percent change. This near equivalence can be seen by the following illustration.

The rate of return on a stock not paying dividends is defined as:

$$\text{Return} = (\text{Ending Price} - \text{Beginning Price})/\text{Beginning Price}$$

Normally, the return is expressed in percent, which is accomplished by multiplying the result of the above equation by 100.

Using \$1.10 as the ending price and \$1.00 as the beginning price, we can calculate the rate of return as:

$$\text{Return} = (1.10 - 1.00) / 1.00$$
$$= 0.10$$

To express 0.10 in percent, we multiply 0.10 by 1.00 and obtain a return of 10 percent.

We can perform the same calculation in natural logarithms, with only a slight modification.

$$\text{Return} = \text{Nat. Log (Ending Price)} - \text{Nat. Log (Beginning Price)}$$
$$= \text{Nat. Log} (1.10) - \text{Nat. Log} (1.00)$$
$$= 0.10 - 0.00$$
$$= 0.10$$

Taking the differences in successive items in a price series is called *taking first differences*. If we take first differences in the logarithms of monthly prices of a stock, we obtain a series of monthly rates of return based on price and excluding dividend.

Natural logarithms have several advantages:

1. First differences in the natural logs of prices are rates of return.

2. The data is homogenized, since the differences no longer depend on the level of prices.

3. The distribution of first differences in the logs of prices is more approximately normal than first differences in the original prices.

It is also useful to know that the following two expressions are equivalent:

$$\text{Nat. Log (Ending Price)} - \text{Nat. Log (Beginning Price)}$$
$$= \text{Nat. Log (Ending Price/Beginning Price)}$$

Examples of natural logs are shown in Table 2.2.

Summary

The standard deviation can be used to measure the variability of a set of numbers. The standard deviation determines the shape of the normal curve, and the normal curve approximates first differences in the natural logarithms of stock prices. By using these three measures—the standard deviation, the normal curve, and natural logarithms—we can derive probability estimates of the future.

Table 2.2   Examples of Natural Logarithms

Number	Natural Logarithm
0.85	-0.16
0.90	-0.11
1.00	0.00
1.05	0.05
1.10	0.10
1.15	0.14
1.20	0.18

CHAPTER 3

The Statistical Basis for Estimating Future Probable Changes in Stock Prices

If you know that the distribution of changes in a series is normal and if you know the standard deviation, you can make probability estimates of the future. Though the distribution of stock price changes is *not* normal, we can perform the log transformation to make it approximately normal. Moreover, the standard deviation for differences in (the logs of) stock prices rises in a regular way, so if we know the standard deviation for one time interval, we can compute it for any other time interval.

Figure 3.1 shows the monthly closing price of the Standard & Poor's 500 from 1871 to 1991. This index combines the Cowles Common Stock index, which covers the years through 1937, and the Standard & Poor's 500 Index, which began in 1938.

Figure 3.1 has several significant features:

1. The index rose substantially over the period. In 1871, the index was 4.44, and by the end of 1991, it had reached 388.50. Although that seems to be a substantial rise, it represents an average annual compound growth of only 3.8 percent.

2. The series exhibits considerable fluctuation. The degree of fluctuation appears to be much greater in the latter part of the period, on the right side of the figure.

We can examine the degree of fluctuation in greater detail by plotting the monthly changes in the index instead of the index itself. Figure 3.2 shows the monthly changes in price beginning in 1871 and ending in 1991. Each bar on the figure shows the dollar rise or fall in price during that month.

**Figure 3.1   1871–1991 Standard & Poor's 500
Monthly Closing Price**

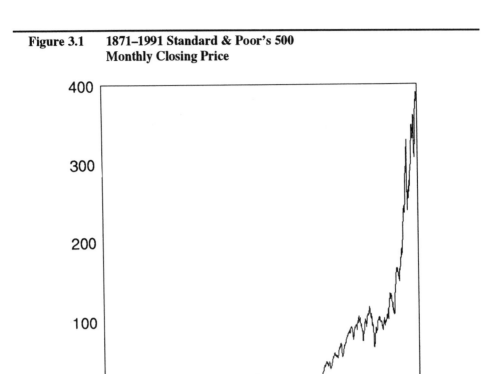

Figure 3.2 also has some significant features. Increases and decreases in the index occur regularly throughout the period, more or less at random. Scanning the figure, it is very difficult to ascertain whether the next change will be up or down. The data is highly random; there seem to be nearly as many decreases as increases. In fact, there are more increases than decreases: 56 percent versus 43 percent.

Another significant feature of Figures 3.1 and 3.2 is that, in each, the degree of fluctuation appears to be much higher in the latter part of the period, when the price of the Standard & Poor's 500 was much higher. The fact that the degree of fluctuation was much higher at high levels of the index shows that the degree of change in the index was proportional to the level of the index. In other words, the probability of a $1 change when the index was $10 might be the same as the probability of a $10 change when the index was $100. Whenever the index changes substantially, estimates of the degree of change depend on the level of the index.

We need some way to remove the influence of the effect of the level of the index on the degree of change. An appropriate method is to convert the index to natural logarithms. Figure 3.3 plots the same index, the Standard & Poor's 500, but records the natural logarithms of the index instead of the original index. The figure shows clearly how the influence of the level of rates was removed by using the measure of natural logarithms.

**Figure 3.2   1871–1991 Standard & Poor's 500
Monthly Change in Price**

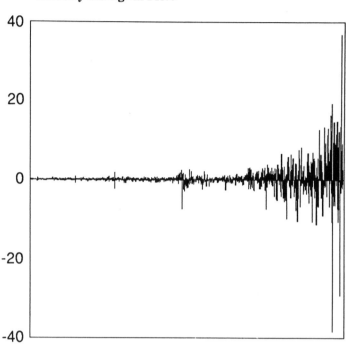

As can be seen in Figure 3.3, the sharp difference between the initial and final values has disappeared. The index still rises, but the degree of fluctuation is relatively consistent throughout, as we would expect from a log transformation.

First differences in the logarithms give a truer picture of the degree of variation than the logarithms themselves. Figure 3.4 shows monthly changes in the natural logarithms of the Standard & Poor's 500 Index. It has been derived from the underlying data of Figure 3.3 but now depicts first differences in the logarithms of prices instead of the logarithms of prices.

Figure 3.4 reveals a striking and important point. There is no longer any trend in the degree of fluctuation in the Standard & Poor's 500 Index. The conversion to natural logarithms has removed the effect of the level of price on the degree of fluctuation; the monthly differences in the logs of prices shown in Figure 3.4 are roughly the same over the entire span of years, 1871–1991.

The significant point illustrated by Figure 3.4 is that, in studying fluctuations in stock prices, we should homogenize the data by taking the logs of the original prices. By doing so, we eliminate the scaling effect caused by the particular level of the index. In homogenizing the data, we used the natural logarithms of the index instead of the index itself. The first differences in the logs were, for the most part, equally volatile throughout the entire century.

Figure 3.3   1871–1991 Standard & Poor's 500
Natural Logarithm of Price

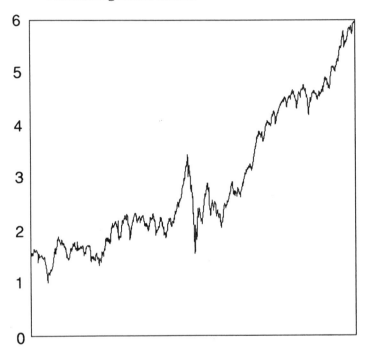

The Effect of the Time Interval Used
in Calculating the Standard Deviation

For random series, the standard deviation rises with the square root of the difference interval, or holding period. In Figure 3.3, we graphed changes in the Standard & Poor's 500 over one-month intervals. We can compute the standard deviation of the one-month changes as a measure of the monthly volatility. This will give us a one-month standard deviation. We can also take two-month changes and compute the two-month standard deviation. In the same way, we can compute the three-month standard deviation, the four-month standard deviation, the five-month standard deviation (and so on) for three-month, four-month, and five-month time-difference intervals.

In a purely random series, the standard deviation will rise with the square root of the differencing interval—in this case, the number of months. That means that we will get a series such as that shown in Table 3.1, where s_1 is the *one*-month standard deviation and s_t is the standard deviation over t months.

For common stock prices, the standard deviation increases approximately with the square root of the differencing interval, or holding period. Figure 3.5 shows that relationship for the standard deviation of changes in the logs of the Standard & Poor's 500 Index from 1871 to 1991.

Figure 3.4   **1871–1991 Standard & Poor's 500**
Change in Logarithm of Price

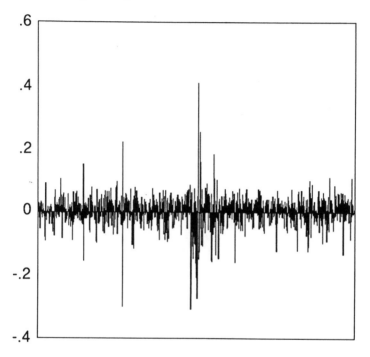

Table 3.1   **Standard Deviation of a Random Series**

Interval in Months	Standard Deviation s_t		
1	1	×	s_1
2	1.41	×	s_1
3	1.73	×	s_1
4	2	×	s_1
9	3	×	s_1
16	4	×	s_1
25	5	×	s_1

In Figure 3.5, the standard deviation rises with increases in the difference interval (the number of months). The relationship is not perfect, but it approximates the square-root-of-time rule. The slope is 0.48, just under the square root value of 0.50, and the relationship is highly significant, with a coefficient of correlation of 0.99. We can use this relationship

**Figure 3.5   Standard Deviation vs. Time Interval
S&P 500 Price Index, Monthly 1871–1991**

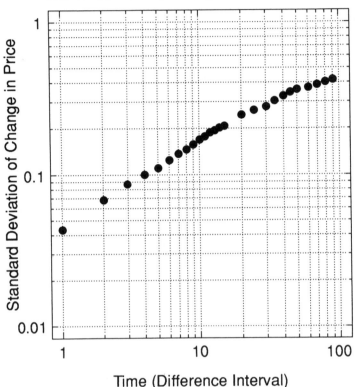

to estimate the standard deviation and use it to model the distribution of price changes for various time intervals, from one day to five to 10 years, given the fact that the distribution of changes in the logs of stock prices is approximately normal.

Figure 3.6 gives a histogram of the distribution of monthly changes in the logs of the Standard & Poor's 500. The distribution is bell-shaped: high at the center and thin, with wide tails. It is only approximately normal but sufficiently so that we can use the normal distribution to make probability estimates of the future.

Summary

For a major stock price index, you can homogenize the data by taking first differences in the natural logarithms of price. In doing so, you obtain a measure of volatility that does not depend on how high or low the index is or from what historical period the index is drawn. There are some exceptions, of course, such as the aberrations of 1929 and 1987.

For a stock price series, the measure of volatility, the standard deviation, rises roughly with the square root of the holding period, or time. The square-root-of-time relationship

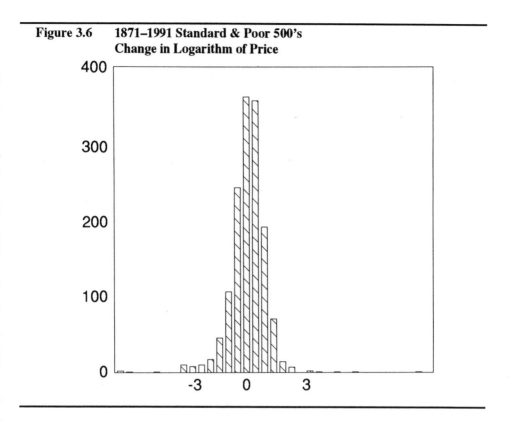

**Figure 3.6   1871–1991 Standard & Poor 500's
Change in Logarithm of Price**

makes it possible to estimate the standard deviation for any length period, provided you know it for one period. If the distribution is normal and we know the standard deviation, we can calculate probable changes. The distribution of changes in the logs of prices is bell-shaped and approximately normal.

We have just described the foundation for the method of estimating probable changes in the prices of the stock market. The same method will work for many other economic series, from company revenues to company profits and losses.

CHAPTER 4

How Knowing the Probability Can Improve Your Investment Decisions

If we could predict a specific event—such as how high the price of Microsoft will go next week or how low profit margins will fall next year—we could become very rich. Unfortunately, no one's financial crystal ball is good enough to make specific predictions.

Even though we can't predict the *specific,* we can do the next best thing: predict the *probability.* We can do that because changes in (the logs of) stock prices and other financial variables, though random, are nevertheless distributed in a way that can be modeled by the laws of probability.

Knowing the probability, then, can be very helpful in solving a wide range of problems, as illustrated in the following examples. Later on, we will show how to estimate probabilities to help address specific investment situations more profitably.

Investment Problem 1

Whether to Buy a Bond Now—or Wait

John Ames had money to invest. He wanted to buy long-term bonds because he wouldn't need the money for 10 years. But he wanted and needed the income. Rates on 10-year bonds were 8 percent. His investment adviser told him that rates would rise to 10 percent within the next year and to wait until they did before buying long-bonds.

John did some hard thinking: "If my adviser is absolutely correct, and there is a 100 percent probability of an increase, then I should wait. But if the advice is not very certain, then I should not wait."

John wanted more certainty, so he went to another adviser and asked how likely it was that rates would reach 10 percent. That adviser said: "The probability is very low. Only 3 percent. And there's an equal probability that rates could drop to 6.4 percent."

Knowing that there is a probability of only 3 percent that 10-year bond rates will rise to 10 percent was enough for John. He decided that the odds were too low. He also didn't want to be faced with lower rates. So he bought the 10-year bonds.

Knowing the probability that rates would rise a given amount enabled John to make an informed decision on bond investment.

Investment Problem 2

How to Estimate Whether a Firm Will Be Profitable

Dick Jensen wanted to buy a company that he could own and manage himself. After a long search, he had narrowed his choice to Crick Electronics, and one other. Crick had an exciting product, served a growing industry, and was cheap.

There was only one problem. The firm had lost money in two of the past five years. Dick did not want to have a problem company, and he was concerned that Crick might have losses in the future. He would not want to buy unless the company was reasonably sure of being profitable.

The seller, Mr. Harris, assured Dick that there would be no future losses. "The odds of a future loss are less than 1 in 1,000," he affirmed. "We have corrected the problems that made us lose money in the past."

If Harris was anywhere near right, Dick would buy. But were the odds really 1 in 1,000?

Dick decided to ask his accountant's advice. The accountant calculated the probability of Crick suffering a future loss. The accountant derived the probability from the standard deviation of past changes in earnings, the current level of earnings, and the normal probability distribution.

The accountant's answer was not at all what Dick expected. "The probability of a future loss," said the accountant, "is 40 percent."

Dick initially questioned the calculation, but when he understood how it was done, he accepted the result. With the prospect of that high probability of loss, Dick decided to pass on Crick, knowing that the low price reflected the risk. He turned to his second choice, which turned out to be a good buy.

Knowing the probability that a firm will lose money in the future can help you decide whether you want to buy or not buy.

Investment Problem 3

How Likely Is the Dividend to Be Cut?

Skip Johnson had picked a stock, Xron, primarily on the basis of its dividend yield. Of course, he also was interested in potential price appreciation, since Xron was in a growth industry, had a solid niche in the market, and was considered well managed.

But what especially interested Skip Johnson was the 10 percent dividend yield. His main concern was that the dividend might be cut. When he asked his broker about this, his answer was prompt: "Of course not, there is less than 1 chance in 100 they'll cut the dividend. Don't give it a thought."

Wanting to be sure, Skip asked a financial analyst what the likelihood was the dividend would be cut.

The analyst said that the probability could be estimated from the payout ratio. Skip listened carefully as the analyst explained the procedure. The probability of a cut surprised him—it was an astounding 70 percent.

"That's a long way from 1 in 100," he mused to himself. Skip did not buy the stock, but he did get another broker.

Investment Problem 4

The Odds of a Rise in Margins

Jack Kirby wanted to expand his company, Melor Radio, into a new market. Adding a second radio station in a neighboring state would give him much broader coverage. To make the purchase, Jack had to be able to meet the interest charges on the debt he must incur. The price of the station seemed too high to do that, unless its profit margins could be raised. Current operating margins on the new station were 20 percent against a national average of 30 percent. Jack felt that if he could raise margins to 30 percent, he then could afford to make the purchase at an acceptable price.

But could he increase margins that much? He asked his accountant what the odds were of getting to the higher margin. The accountant figured what costs might be cut to come up with an estimate. After a week of going over the data, she calculated he might get to 30 percent if all possible cuts were made and everything worked out right, including no softening in the local or national markets.

Then as a check, the accountant estimated the probability of getting to 30 percent by using a different method: looking at past changes in margins.

After completing the analysis, she brought the results to Jack.

"Based on past changes in margins," she said, "the probability of reaching 30 percent is about 1 in 5—a 20 percent probability."

Jack pondered this information for some time and then decided to lower his bid, giving himself a greater margin of safety. Frankly, he didn't like the odds. Lowering the bid would make it possible to do the deal with margins lower than 30 percent.

The next day Jack's lower bid won, thanks to his accountant's probability estimate. He was able to increase margins to the lower target of 26 percent and pay off the loan.

Investment Problem 5

Which Stock Will Have the Higher Future Yield?

Terry Haynes wanted to know whether, five years from now, the stock yielding 4 percent today would have a higher yield, based on today's price and the future dividend, than the stock yielding 8 percent. Current wisdom seemed to indicate that the lower-yielding stock was in a faster-growing company.

When he asked a friend in the investment business about the choices, he was told that the 4 percent stock would likely have a higher yield in the future, but it might take more than five years.

Another friend was more definite: "Certainly," he said, "the 4 percent yield will be higher."

Not satisfied with this advice, Terry turned to a statistician, who proceeded to calculate the probability. "The probability is only 10 percent that the lower-yield stock will have a higher yield five years from now. Both yields," he added, "are based on present price."

When it was explained to him, Terry saw how the statistician had derived the probability and he accepted it. He wanted the higher income, but he became even more intrigued by the price appreciation prospects of the lower-yielding stock. He decided to take a chance on it, even though the income, now and in the future, would probably be much lower.

Summary

These examples illustrate how knowing the probability can help provide a more informed decision. Later on, we'll describe how to calculate probability for various investment problems. But first, we'll describe some of the underlying characteristics of stock prices, earnings, and other financial variables.

CHAPTER 5

The Dispersion of Stock Prices

On a stock trade, it's logical to expect that the price rise anticipated by the buyer will equal the price decline anticipated by the seller. Since the opposing views offset each other, the probability of a rise or fall in price is the same. For a stock market, such as the New York Stock Exchange, where buyers and sellers congregate and trades take place, we can describe the expected change (in the log of price) as:

$$E \left(\Delta \log_e \text{price} \right) = 0 \qquad (5.1)$$

In this case and if the trades are independent in a probability sense, as they may be expected to be, then we may expect the following: the distribution of changes in the logs of prices will be normal and have a mean of zero and a dispersion that increases with the square root of the number of transactions.

If transactions occur evenly over time, as they do on average, then dispersion will increase with the square root of time. We measure dispersion by the standard deviation of changes in the logs of prices, as follows:

$$\text{Standard Deviation } t \text{ Intervals } = \text{Standard Deviation } 1 \text{ Interval} \times t^{0.5} \qquad (5.2)$$

The *Central Limit Theorem* implies that the distribution of sums of (the logs of) price changes will approach a normal distribution for large numbers of transactions, whatever the distribution of the individual price changes.

The first person to examine the distribution of changes in stock prices was M. F. M. Osborne. Osborne looked at the distribution of price changes, defined as the first difference in the logs of prices. He found that the distribution was approximately normal and that the standard deviation of first differences in the logs of stock prices increased with the square root of the differencing interval.

Osborne's discovery had two important results:

1.   It provided evidence that first differences in the logs of stock prices were random and had a normal distribution and a zero mean.

2.   It furnished a rule for estimating the standard deviation for one time interval from data of another time interval by application of the square-root-of-time rule.

Tables 5.1 and 5.2 show the results of tests of the square root rule. The procedure used was to compute the standard deviation of 1-day changes in a stock price index and then use the square root rule to estimate the standard deviation for 2-day, 4-day, 8-day, 16-day, 32-day, 64-day, and 128-day intervals. Then, actual standard deviations were computed for each time interval, and the actual standard deviations were compared with the estimated standard deviations. The results are shown in Tables 5.1 and 5.2 for a stock index and a single stock, respectively.

Table 5.1 records the standard deviation of daily changes in the logs of the Standard & Poor's 500 Index from 1982 to mid-1993. The standard deviation for changes in price are shown over eight intervals: 1, 2, 4, 8, 16, 32, 64, and 128 days.

In Table 5.1, the formula for estimating the standard deviation is given in columns 2, 3, and 4. The expected standard deviation is obtained by multiplying the standard deviation for one day by the square root of the number of days. The standard deviation for one day is 1.05. To obtain the value for four days, we multiply 1.05 by the square root of 4, or by 2, and obtain 2.1. The estimated value 2.1 is shown in the next-to-last column. It compares with the actual value of 2.1, given in the last column.

The actual figures are the standard deviation of the changes in logs. We've arbitrarily multiplied the values by 100, which makes them comparable to the standard deviation of

Table 5.1	1982–1993 Standard & Poor's 500 Changes in the Logs of Daily Prices (x 100)				
Time Interval in Days	Square Root of Time Interval		Standard Deviation of 1 Day (x 100)	Estimated Standard Deviation (x 100)	Actual Standard Deviation (x 100)
1	1	×	1.05 =	1.0	1.0
2	1.4	×	1.05 =	1.5	1.5
4	2	×	1.05 =	2.1	2.1
8	2.8	×	1.05 =	3.0	2.9
16	4	×	1.05 =	4.2	4.0
32	5.7	×	1.05 =	5.9	5.5
64	8	×	1.05 =	8.4	7.8
128	11.3	×	1.05 =	11.9	10.3

Table 5.2	General Motors Common Stock, 1982–1993 Changes in the Logs of Daily Prices (x 100)				
Time Interval in Days	Square Root of Time Interval		Standard Deviation of 1 Day (x 100)	Estimated Standard Deviation (x 100)	Actual Standard Deviation (x 100)
1	1	×	1.81 =	1.8	1.8
2	1.4	×	1.81 =	2.6	2.5
4	2	×	1.81 =	3.6	3.4
8	2.8	×	1.81 =	5.1	4.7
16	4	×	1.81 =	7.2	6.6
32	5.7	×	1.81 =	10.2	9.4
64	8	×	1.81 =	14.5	13.3
128	11.3	×	1.81 =	20.5	17.7

the percentage change in price. For changes under 15 percent, 100 times the log change is not far from the percentage change.

We can see by comparing the last two columns of Table 5.1 that the estimated and actual standard deviations are quite close. For the 2-day and 4-day intervals, they are the same. For longer intervals, the estimated and actual standard deviations differ slightly.

The close correspondence shows that the square root rule is quite accurate. Not only that, but the fact that the standard deviation rises with the square root of time provides evidence that first differences in the logs of stock prices exhibit the characteristics of a random variable.

Table 5.2 gives the estimated and actual standard deviation of first differences in the logs of the price of General Motors stock from 1982 to mid-1993. The standard deviation of the 1-day difference was 0.0181, which, when multiplied by 100, is 1.81. We used that figure to derive the estimated standard deviation for 2-day, 3-day, and up to 128-day intervals. The estimated standard deviations are shown in the fourth column of Table 5.2; the actual standard deviations are shown in the fifth column. We can clearly see a fairly close correspondence between the estimated and actual standard deviations for this individual stock.

Summary

What is the significance of the square-root-of-time rule for the investor? It has two important implications:

1.   We can predict risk as measured by the standard deviation. We can estimate the standard deviation for alternate time intervals if we know it for one time interval. For example, if we know the standard deviation for weekly periods, we can estimate it for monthly periods; if we know it for annual periods, we can estimate it for five-year or possibly 10-year periods. The estimates are not perfect, but they are reasonably approximate. Statisticians will warn against extrapolating beyond the period for which we have data. To calculate a standard deviation for a month, we need nearly a year of data, and for a decade, we need eight to 10 decades of data. Nevertheless, the square root rule seems to hold reasonably well. The rule has been tested on other kinds of series, including corporate earnings, dividends, and U.S. bond yields, as shown in Appendix VII, Figure VII.1.

2.   Although the absolute variability of stock returns (measured by the standard deviation) rises with the square root of time, the standard deviation of the *mean return* declines with the square root of time. Put another way, the standard deviation of the total return rises with time, but the standard deviation of the *mean* declines with time. For example, while there may be great variability in our total return on a stock over a 10-year interval, the average variability will be low.

The square root rule is important because it provides evidence of the random character of changes in stock prices. When we define *risk* as the standard deviation, the rule enables us to predict risk for different lengths of periods. It shows us how the risks of the stock market as a whole, and of individual stocks, in particular, change with time.

The probable gains and losses of investing in stocks, described in later tables, will depend on the standard deviation. So the ability to predict the standard deviation for different time, or holding, intervals is crucial to assessing probable gains and losses.

CHAPTER 6

The Basic Model of the Stock Market

In Chapter 3, we demonstrated that transforming stock prices into the natural logarithms (i.e., $\log_e$) of stock prices created a series in which the variations in price were not directly related to the level of price. First differences in the logs of prices were more or less homogeneous, unlike first differences in the prices themselves, which reflect the level of prices. We also showed that the distribution of first differences in the logs of prices was approximately normal with a zero mean. The probability of an increase in stock prices was the same as the probability of a decrease. Finally, we showed that the standard deviation of differences in the logs of prices increased with the square root of time. First differences in the logs of stock prices are equivalent to percentage changes using continuous compounding or to growth rates.

If you know one stock price, you can guess fairly well the next stock price will be of the same general magnitude, or a number close to the one you know. You don't know whether it will be higher or lower, but you know that it will be in the same neighborhood.

But knowing the first difference in the log of price, the return over the most recent period, gives you little help in knowing what the next first difference in logs will be. You can't tell whether it will be positive or negative, or how large it will be. The past change tells you little about the future change. But, if you have a lot of past changes in the logs, and plot their distribution, you can make probability estimates about the next change. You can say that the probability is that it will be positive (generally a 50% probability), that it will be more than 0.1, or 0.2, or whatever. Or, less than -0.1. This is the same kind of statement that we make about light in quantum theory. We can state the probability that a particle of light will strike a certain point after it passes through a small slit, for light, like stock prices, diffuses.

It is important to note that the *differences over time intervals* in the logs of stock prices are random, not the logs of stock prices and not the prices themselves. The distinction between the prices (or the logs in prices) and changes in prices (or the logs in prices) is important. The cumulative sum of first differences in the logs of prices results in the logs of prices, a series that forms a random walk. Imagine the path of a drunkard walking over a plane. We know something about the position of the drunk from his last position, but we do not know the direction of his next step.

We can summarize the above characteristics of stock prices as follows:

1. First differences in the logs of stock prices for any stock form a random series, and have a mean of zero and an approximately normal distribution.

2. The standard deviation of differences with time in the logs of stock prices rises with the square root of the time differencing interval. This holds for the standard deviation of differences in the logs of a single stock; it also holds for the cross-section standard deviation of differences in the logs of prices for a portfolio of stocks. (The cross-section standard deviation refers to the dispersion of changes among a sample of different stocks, the range encompassed by the middle two-thirds of the stocks.)

3. While the *median* change in the price in $ of a stock, or a portfolio of stocks, is zero, the *average* change of the portfolio (but not of the individual stock) will be positive and, assuming that the stock price series is continuous in price, can be calculated from the cross-section standard deviation, as shown later in this chapter.

All of the above characteristics of stock prices, except for the calculation of the mean change, were first described by M.F.M. Osborne in 1959 in a classic paper titled "Brownian Motion in the Stock Market." In 1900, Bachelier was the first to describe a financial series as random and having a normal distribution of zero mean and a dispersion (square root of variance of time difference) that increased with the square root of the time interval; Bachelier's analysis, which was applied to prices of French bonds, went unrecognized for its importance for a half century. But Bachelier's work predated Einstein's similar paper on Brownian motion by a half dozen years.

The above characteristics of stock prices enable us to do the following:

1. Estimate the mean expected rise in the market, in a single stock, or in a portfolio of stocks.

2. Determine the risk in a stock or portfolio of stocks over any interval of time if you know the risk (mean standard deviation) in a single interval.

3. Estimate the distribution of assets within a portfolio of originally equally weighted stocks after any interval of time.

4. Estimate the probability of a rise (or fall) of any magnitude or more after any particular time interval.

Some of these estimates will be covered in this chapter; others will be treated in later chapters.

A useful way of viewing changes in stock prices is to think of a matrix of so many rows and so many columns, like an expanded checkerboard. Consider that, in each box, or at each intersection of row and column, there is a random variable that has a zero mean and a normal distribution. Let each column represent a different time sequential date, **t,** and each row a different stock, **s(j).** Each of the random variables is independent.

In addition, let there be a single row, called the market row, m, also composed of random variables. Each of these variables has a zero mean and a normal distribution, and each is independent of the others in the same row.

We can generate this kind of matrix by flipping coins, assigning +1 to heads and -1 to tails, so that the random variable in each box represents the sum of flips for one day, or for one week, on a specific stock. After a given number of coin tosses, this process would generate random variables with a normal distribution and zero mean.

Now suppose that we add the market row to each of the stock rows so that, in each box on the checkerboard, we have the sum of two random variables: one representing the market return in that time interval and the other representing that particular stock's return in that time interval. If we then add the market random number to the stock random number, we will create a new random number, the sum of the stock and market numbers. We might call this the combined matrix, that is, the matrix that combines the stock and market components.

Osborne, who postulated this model, used copper coins to represent the stock component and a gold coin to represent the market component. With 1,000 stocks, you would need 1,000 copper coins to generate the 1,000 rows of the stock matrix, one coin for each row, plus one gold coin to generate the market row. For the combined matrix, the random number in each box would represent the sum of the market gold coin and the stock copper coin in that particular time interval.

This model has some interesting features. Looking at the combined matrix only, the numbers for all stocks in a particular time interval (the same column), **t,** will be similar in that each stock will have the same market component added to it. That common influence reflects the tendency of all stocks in the real world to move together in the same direction, up or down. If the market is up, or particularly substantially up, most stocks will be up, and vice versa.

The numbers in each column, or in the same time interval, are not the same due to the random number, the copper coin, peculiar to that stock in that time interval. Thus, for any particular time interval (one column), we have a column of numbers that move together in part but also are dispersed or spread out. Under the coin model, the dispersion will approximate the normal distribution, which is the same distribution that characterizes returns on stocks. The components peculiar to the stocks, the 1,000 copper coins, are independent of each other.

The degree of dispersion across stocks (measured by the standard deviation) in any time interval will be directly related to the square root of the length of the time interval. The square-root-of-time rule holds in the real world.

Another feature of the combined matrix is that what happens in one column, or one time interval, is unrelated to what happens in the next column, or time interval. Not only are the market variables in separate time intervals independent of each other, but the stock variables (i.e., the stock components) are independent of each other, as well. This is also true in the real world.

Next, suppose we sum each column and divide the sum by the number of stocks in each column, in this case, 1,000. Doing so will give us the mean for each column. The mean is nearly directly comparable to changes in the market average (or would be, were market averages composed of portfolios in which each stock had the same weight or market value).

The mean has several important features. It is a random variable, since it represents the sum of a column of random variables. It is very nearly identical to the market row, described earlier. Nearly all of the variance in the mean (in one column) comes from the market component, the gold coin. This phenomenon is reflected in the real world. Since the stock component and the market component have the same variance, as they do in the coin model, an individual stock will have twice the variance of the market. Osborne showed this to be the case. The underlying reason for diversifying an investment into a number of stocks is to eliminate the variance arising from the stock component and thereby reduce the portfolio variance to that of the market.

The evidence for the presence of a market component is that, as the number of stocks in a market average increases to a very large number, say 500 or 1,000, the variance of changes in the market average does not decline to zero as it would if were there no market component. The variance of changes in the average declines to about half of what it is for a typical stock, and that is the basis for concluding that the market average, the gold coin, contributes about half of the stocks' total variance. All of these phenomena were shown statistically by Osborne.

The combined matrix that we have described refers not to stock prices or to dollar changes in stock prices or even to percentage changes in stock prices. Rather, the model reflects changes in the logs of stock prices. It is changes in the logs of stock prices that are responsible for the upward movement in dollars of the market average at about 5 percent per year. The distribution of log changes in prices is normal, which means the distribution is symmetrical about a mean of zero. The distribution of percentage changes, however, is skewed in the positive direction, so that positive percentage changes are larger, on average, than negative percentage changes (even though positive and negative log changes tend to be the same). This may sound contradictory, but it is a mathematical and empirical fact.

Illogical as it may seem, it is also true that both buyer and seller may be expected to gain when outcomes are measured in dollars or shares. Both could not gain as the result of a single trial, but as the result of repeated, independent trials not overlapping in time. However, when gains are measured by changes in logarithm of price, or logarithm of the number of shares, the expected gain of each is zero. Both of these features were pointed out by Osborne.

The model we have just described is a simplified version of the real world of stock prices. It is an approximate description of the real world. While the model describes the impact of the stock market on changes in the price of an individual stock, there are many other influences that should be taken into account, such as the influence of industry factors. The model could be modified to include such things as the influence of particular industries. In addition, changes occur from one historical era to the next in the volatility not only of the market but also in the volatility of individual stocks.

An Illustration

We can illustrate this model with the following example. Table 6.1 gives the closing prices of 10 stocks from 1981 to 1991. The prices have been rounded to whole dollar amounts. Table 6.2 gives for each stock first differences in natural logs of prices (shown in Table 6.1) from one year to the next. The first differences in the logs have been multiplied by 100; they represent rates of return in log terms. The first line of Table 6.3 gives the yearly first differences in the natural logs of the Standard & Poor's 500. The remaining rows of Table 6.3 give the stock's first difference in logs less the S&P first differences in logs. The data in Table 6.3 were obtained by subtracting the S&P line from each line of Table 6.2. Thus, Table 6.3 represents the stock component of the rate of return for each stock.

For example, the price of Abbott was $7 at the close of 1981 and $10 at the close of 1982 (as shown in the upper left-hand part of Table 6.1). The natural log of 7 is .84 and the natural log of 10 is 1.00. The difference (1.00 − .84) is .36. 100 times .36 is 36 (as shown in the upper left portion of Table 6.2). The change in natural logs (x100) of 36 corresponds to a percentage change of 43 percent. The S&P in the same time interval declined, with a first difference in the natural logs of .10, which times 100 is -10. If we subtract the -10 from 36 (36 − 10) we obtain 46. The number 46 is given in the upper left portion of Table 6.3.

These tables (6.1, 6.2, and 6.3) are a representation of the model just described. Table 6.2 is the combined matrix, which gives the return for each stock. Table 6.3 shows the stock return less the market return (expressed in first differences in logs x100). Thus, Table 6.2 represents the sums of the gold and copper coins; Table 6.3 represents only the copper coin.

Table 6.1   Closing Prices of Selected Stocks, 1981–1991

Closing Price in Nearest Whole Dollar

Stock	1981	1982	1983	1984	1985	1986	1987	1988	1989	1990	1991
Abbott	7	10	11	10	17	23	24	24	34	45	69
Alcoa	26	31	45	37	39	34	47	56	75	58	64
Amax	47	22	24	16	14	12	20	23	23	21	20
Amdahl	7	7	9	7	7	12	18	20	14	14	16
Amer Expr	11	16	16	19	27	28	23	27	35	21	21
CBS	47	60	66	72	116	127	157	171	188	173	143
Chase	27	25	23	24	36	36	22	29	35	11	17
Chem Bank	24	27	29	35	45	42	21	31	30	11	21
Chevron	43	32	35	31	38	45	40	46	68	73	69
Chrysler	2	8	12	14	21	25	22	26	19	13	12

**Table 6.2   First Differences in Natural Logarithms of Selected Stocks
1981–82 to 1990–91**

**First Difference in Natural Logs of Price (x 100)
Equals Rate of Return in Natural Logs (x 100)**

Stock	81-82	82-83	83-84	84-85	85-86	86-87	87-88	88-89	89-90	90-91
Abbott	36	10	-10	53	30	4	0	35	28	43
Alcoa	18	37	-20	5	-14	32	18	29	-26	10
Amax	-76	9	-41	-13	-15	51	14	0	-9	-5
Amdahl	0	25	-25	0	54	41	11	-36	0	13
Amer Expr	37	0	17	35	4	-20	16	26	-51	0
CBS	24	10	9	48	9	21	9	9	-8	-19
Chase	-8	-8	4	41	0	-49	28	19	-116	44
Chem Bank	12	7	19	25	-7	-69	39	-3	-100	65
Chevron	-30	9	-12	20	17	-12	14	39	7	-6
Chrysler	139	41	15	41	17	-13	17	-31	-38	-8

**Table 6.3   First Differences in Natural Logarithms of Selected Stocks
Less First Differences in Logs of S&P 500**

Minus First Difference in Logs of S&P 500 (x 100)

S&P 500	-10	14	16	1	23	14	2	12	24	-7

Equals Stock Price Change Less S&P 500 Price Change (x 100)

Stock	81-82	82-83	83-84	84-85	85-86	86-87	87-88	88-89	89-90	90-91
Abbott	46	-4	-26	52	7	-10	-2	23	4	50
Alcoa	28	23	-36	4	-37	18	16	17	-50	17
Amax	-66	-5	-57	-14	-38	37	12	-12	-33	2
Amdahl	10	11	-41	-1	31	27	9	-48	-24	20
Amer Expr	47	-14	1	34	-19	-34	14	14	-75	7
CBS	34	-4	-7	47	-14	7	7	-3	-32	-12
Chase	2	-22	-12	40	-23	-63	26	7	-140	51
Chem Bank	22	-7	3	24	-30	-83	37	-15	-124	72
Chevron	-20	-5	-28	19	-6	-26	12	27	-17	1
Chrysler	149	27	-1	40	-6	-27	15	-43	-62	-1

The Model

We can summarize Osborne's model in the following way:

Changes in the price of a stock may be represented as the (antilogs of the) sum of two independent random elements: one peculiar to the stock, the other to the market. The expected value of these elements is zero, and the standard deviation is about the same for each, roughly 18 percent per year.

For a portfolio, the variance of changes in the natural logarithms of the mean is equal to the variance of the changes in the natural logarithms of the market plus $1/n$ times the variance of changes in the natural logarithms of the stock components where **n** is the number of stocks in the portfolio. We can designate the portfolio's variance as s_p^2, the market variance (the variance of the S&P 500, for example) as s_m^2, and the stock component variance as s_s^2. Then, we can compute the variance of the portfolio:

Portfolio Variance = Market Variance + Stock Component Variance/**n**

or

$$s_p^{\,2} = s_m^{\,2} + s_s^{\,2} / n \tag{6.1}$$

The mean change in the market is given by the exponent of $s^2/2$:

$$\text{Mean Change} = \exp(s^2/2) \tag{6.2}$$

The variance of the mean change in Equation (6.2) is:

$$\text{Variance of the Mean Change} = \exp(4 s^2/2)$$

The effect of the time interval, or holding period, is:

$$s(t) = s(1) t^{0.5} \tag{6.3}$$

In the above equations, s is the standard deviation of changes in the logs of price of the stock, the market value of the portfolio, or the market in general, and s^2 is the variance of those items. Furthermore:

s_s is the standard deviation peculiar to the stock (a single row);

s_m is the standard deviation peculiar to the market (the single market row);

s_p is the standard deviation of the portfolio;

$s(1)$ is the standard deviation in unit time; and

t   is the interval of time the portfolio is held.

The expected mean of the log differences is zero, and the distribution of changes in the logs is approximately normal.

The distribution has several surprising features, discussed in the following section. First, we can examine the equations in light of the example given in Tables 6.1, 6.2, and 6.3. The first row in Table 6.3 gives returns for the Standard & Poor's 500; the standard deviation of those Standard & Poor's 500 returns (s_m) is 12. The average of the standard deviation of the component peculiar to the stocks (s_s, from Table 6.3) is 36. The mean changes of Table 6.2 for the years 1981–92, 1982–83, . . . ,1990–91 were 15, 14, -4, 25, 9, -1, 17, 9, -31, and 14. The standard deviation of the mean changes (s_p) is 16. If we substitute these numbers in Equation (6.1), we have the following:

$$s_p{}^2 = s_m{}^2 + s_s{}^2 / n$$
$$16^2 = 12^2 + 36^2 / n$$
$$256 = 144 + 130$$
$$256 = 274 \ (\text{approximately})$$

Taking the square roots of 256 and 274, we have

$$16 = 16.6 \ (\text{approximately})$$

The Mean Change

The expected change in the logs of stock prices is zero, yet the expected change in a portfolio of stocks is positive. Similarly, the expected median change in the price of stocks in a portfolio is zero, but the expected average change is positive. This apparent contradiction arises from the fact that when the underlying distribution of the logs is normal with an expected mean of zero, then the approximate mean of the antilogs is positive and can be calculated from Equation (6.2), stated earlier.

This calculation assumes that changes in stock prices are continuous in time. Prices, however, are not continuous: they don't exist between trades, at values less than $1/8, or over the weekend. Consequently, the formula is based on an assumption that is not strictly true. Thus, the results of the calculation are approximate.

In Chapter 15, we show that the cross-sectional standard deviation of annual changes in the logs of all stocks in the New York Stock Exchange from 1926 to 1965 was 0.345, which, according to Equation (6.2) results in an annual average growth of 6.4 percent. In Chapter 7, we use the normal distribution and Equation (6.3) to estimate the distribution of assets of the same New York Stock Exchange stocks, and we then compare that distribution with the actual one.

Risk

Because the part of the change in price due to the stock and the part of the change in price due to the market are independent of each other, we can reduce but not entirely eliminate the risk in a portfolio of stocks. Because components for different stocks tend to be independent, we can reduce the risk of the portfolio mean by increasing the number of stocks in the portfolio. In doing this, we place equal investments in each stock. Because these influences—the stock influence and the market influence—are about the same, we can cut the risk, the standard deviation, *by about half* using a portfolio of a large number of equally weighted stocks. The equation for calculating the reduction in the standard deviation is:

$$s_p^2 = s_m^2 + s_s^2 / n \qquad (6.4)$$

The first term on the right, $s_m 2$, is the market risk, and it never declines. The second term changes when we add stocks. When the number of stocks (**n**) in the portfolio becomes very large, the second term approaches zero and the standard deviation of the total portfolio approaches the standard deviation of the market, s_m.

Modern portfolio theory calls the market risk (s_m) systematic risk because it affects all stocks the same way (i.e., systematically). Market risk, or systematic risk, cannot be reduced by adding additional common stocks. The residual risk attributed to individual stocks can be eliminated entirely by adding enough stocks.

With a large number of stocks, the portfolio risk is:

$$s_p = s_m \qquad (6.4a)$$

The final point to be made is that the standard deviation of returns rises with the square root of the time interval. When we quadruple the holding period, the standard deviation doubles. This fact is revealed by Equation (6.3).

To sum up our discussion of risk, the model says that the standard deviation, s_p, of a portfolio:

1. Declines when we add more stocks to the portfolio;

2. Cannot decline to less than the market standard deviation, s_m; and

3. Increases with the square root of time, or the holding period, **t**.

A Comparison with the Capital Asset Pricing Model

The model we have just described is similar to but significantly different from the Capital Asset Pricing Model (CAPM) originally developed by William Sharpe. The two models are similar in that: each contains a stock component and a market component. Each assumes a normal distribution. Each gives the same weight on average to the stock and market components. Each produces the same reduction in variance with increases in the number of stocks in the portfolio. Each considers (or can consider) as its variables changes in the logs of prices.

The perspective of the two models differs, however. The Sharpe CAPM model postulates a linear relationship between a stock's price changes and the market's price changes, as well as an error term. Thus, a stock's price change consists of a constant peculiar to the stock (the alpha), a factor peculiar to the stock (the beta) times the market change, plus an error term, or a residual, which is random. Thus, the postulated relationship is partly constant (the alpha), partly multiplicative (the beta), partly random, and additive.

The Osborne model, described in this chapter, is totally additive and its two components are both random. There is no constant and no multiplicative factor. A linear relationship is not part of this model.

I had thought that the Sharpe CAPM model would die for lack of evidence, but it has not. However, the constant (the alpha) has been shown to be without significance for stocks. The multiplicative factor (the beta) for a particular stock changes from one period to the next and generally is not significant. For portfolios, however, this is not true, perhaps, in some instances, because of the inclusion of nonstock components in stock portfolios; portfolio betas tend to persist over independent time periods. All in all, one wonders whether it is useful to run linear regressions on what appear to be random data. The whole matter of the Sharpe model has raised considerable debate.

This book employs the Osborne model; in most applications, both models give essentially the same results. This is true, for example, for the effects of diversification, the skewing of portfolios over time, the rise of the standard deviation of changes in stock prices with the difference interval, estimates of market changes over time, and other matters.

Implications of the Model

We will now examine what the Osborne model means for the effect of the number of securities on the risk of a portfolio. We will call the beginning risk 100 for a one-year standard deviation, and we will change only **n**, the number of stocks. As shown in Table 6.4, when the number of stocks is increased from 1 to 2, the standard deviation declines from 100 percent of its original value to 85 percent. With 128 stocks, the standard deviation drops to 54 percent of what it would be with a single stock.

Now we'll examine the effect of the time interval, or holding period, in Equation (6.3) on the standard deviation of a portfolio. We will hold the number of stocks constant and increase the time interval, or holding period (see Table 6.5). As we go from one day to

---

Table 6.4   Implication of the Model for the Effect of Increasing Number of Stocks in a Portfolio on the Standard Deviation of Return

Number of Stocks	1	2	8	16	32	128	inf
Standard Deviation	100	85	68	63	59	54	50

---

four days or from one year to four years, the risk, as measured by the standard deviation of return, doubles.

The third statistical fact mentioned earlier covers the mean. When the distribution of changes is lognormal with an expected mean of zero, the mean of the prices themselves is positive (with the exponent of one-half the standard deviation squared). This seems contradictory, but it is not. Although the mean expected change in the logs is zero, the mean expected change in the actual market is positive and entirely dependent on the standard deviation. This is an important point.

The expected change in the logs of prices is zero, but the expected change in the prices themselves is greater than zero. This apparent contradiction arises because the distribution of changes in stock prices is lognormal; that is, the distribution of changes in the logs of prices is normal. When that is the case, as it is in a portfolio of stocks, the mean change in the log of price is zero, as noted above, but the mean change in the prices in $ is positive.

A rough illustration of this is given by the probability of a price going from $100 to $200 and from $100 to $50. For stock prices, the probability of each is approximately the same. In the first case, the price doubles. In the second, it halves. The change of $\log_e$ from 100 to 200 is +0.69. The change of $\log_e$ from 100 to 50 is -0.69. Consequently, the expected change in logs is the sum of these two values (+0.69 and -0.69), or zero. But the expected change in the antilogs is not zero, as shown in Table 6.6.

The mean change in price is +25, but the mean change in the logs of prices is zero. That illustrates what happens with a lognormal distribution.

We will now examine what the model implies using a (log) standard deviation of 0.35 for a single stock for one year. That's about the same as a standard deviation of 18 percent per year for the market (see Table 6.6).

The data in Table 6.7 illustrate that, if you started with $1 you would expect to have $3.40 at the end of 20 years—an increase arising solely from the fact that the standard deviation of changes in the logs was 0.35, the mean change in logs being zero. The conversion to antilogs causes the rise. While the increase in wealth may seem high, the return is only 6.3 percent per annum compound, which is by no means extraordinary.

Table 6.5   Implication of the Model for the Effect of the Holding Period on the Standard Deviation of Return

Holding Period	1	2	3	4	5	10	20
Standard Deviation	100	141	173	200	224	316	447

Table 6.6   Illustration of Price Changes

Initial Price	Final Price	Price Change	Log Change
$100	$200	+$100	+.69
100	50	-50	-.69

Table 6.7	Implication of the Model for the Expected Value of a Stock Portfolio at the End of Various Number of Years (t) Where the Standard Deviation of the Stock is .35 for a One-Year Interval						
Holding Period Years	1	5	10	20	30	40	50
Expected Value	1.1	1.4	1.8	3.4	6.3	11.6	21.4

Moreover, there is a 50/50 chance that you will have less than $1 at the end of 50 years. And the expected *median* value—as opposed to the expected *mean*—will still be $1.

CHAPTER 7

Predicting the Distribution of Historical Returns on the Stock Market

The measure of market risk—the standard deviation of changes in the log of price—rises with the square root of time. This rule appears to hold for many different time series. It also appears to be invariant—i.e., to hold over different historical eras. The square-root-of-time rule is very useful. If you know the standard deviation for one time-difference interval, you should be able to estimate it for any other time-difference intervals. If you know the standard deviation for daily changes in the Dow Jones Industrial Average, you should be able to calculate the standard deviation for weekly changes, monthly changes, yearly changes, and so on. If you know the standard deviation for a month, you should be able to estimate it for a year or five years.

The distribution of changes in (the logs of) prices is approximately normal. By using the normal distribution as a model, we can then estimate the probable proportion of changes in the market, up or down, of any magnitude or range of magnitudes. We should also be able to estimate the distribution of changes in a market index, such as the Standard & Poor's 500.

Since a large sample of stocks, with the same investment in each, approximates the market to a high degree, we may be able to use the distribution of percentage changes in one market index to approximate that in another market index. In fact, if the measure is truly invariant, we should able to take percentage changes in one stock index, such as the Dow Jones Industrial Average, say over the past four years, and simulate the distribution of percentage changes in another index, say the Standard & Poor's 500 over the last century.

Doing exactly that was the purpose of the following tests. The objective was to demonstrate the similarity of the distributions of percentage changes in the prices of different stock indexes from different historical periods. Table 7.1 presents the results of taking daily changes in the Dow Jones Industrial Average from 1985 to 1989 and using our model of that data to simulate the distribution of daily changes in the same index from 1989 to 1992. Table 7.2 presents the results of taking four years of daily data from the Dow Jones Industrial Average and using the model of that data to simulate the distribution of annual returns of the Standard & Poor's 500 Index over the last 120 years, 1871–1991. Thus, in one test, we tried to describe a distribution in one four-year period based on the distribution in the previous four years. In the other test, we used four years of daily data to estimate the distribution of over a century of annual data for an entirely different index. In the first test, we projected forward; in the second test, we projected backward. If the underlying nature of the data does not change over the course of a century (i.e., if the data is relatively stationary), then it should not matter whether the model is based on data from recent years and backtested on earlier years, or vice versa.

We used the following procedure to do the test:

1. We calculated the standard deviation of daily changes in the logs of stock prices.

2. We assumed that the distribution of changes was (log) normal and had a standard deviation that increased with the square root of time.

3. When we used daily changes in one period to estimate the distribution of daily changes in a subsequent period (Table 7.1), we applied the standard deviation of the first period to the second period, and we used the normal distribution to estimate the proportion of stocks showing each range of percentage changes in the prices of the index.

4. When we used the daily data to estimate the distribution of annual changes, we computed the standard deviation of the daily data and multiplied it by the square root of the number of trading days in a year (250) to obtain the standard deviation of annual percentage changes in the prices of the index. Then we used the normal distribution with that standard deviation to estimate the proportion of stock price change of each range, as shown in Table 7.2.

Why might we expect this to work? Imagine, for a moment, that long-term changes mirror short-term changes for this data. Suppose the distribution of changes is the same, and the degree of change differs only in magnitude. Suppose there is only a change of scale. Suppose in all other respects, things remain the same. If we know what happens to daily changes and we know the rule for converting from daily changes to monthly changes or yearly changes, we can predict the distribution of longer-term changes. We can also predict the probability of a change of any magnitude.

This approach is the precise reverse of Mandelbrot's analysis of fractals. Mandelbrot said that, no matter how small a section of the data we take, that section will resemble the larger section in certain respects. In terms of what was suggested in the last paragraph, reducing the difference interval, in Mandelbrot's view, would have no effect on the results. Here, we argue the reverse: No matter how large the differencing interval, the distribution will be the same, except in terms of scale.

Table 7.1 **Estimation of Daily Changes in Dow Jones Average 1989–1992 Based on Daily Changes 1985–1988**

Percent Change Over	Estimated Proportion	Actual Proportion
-2.3	97	99
-1.8	95	97
-1.0	88	89
0	51	51
1.0	15	11
1.8	5	2
2.3	2	1

Table 7.2 **Estimation of Monthly Changes in S&P 500 1871–1991 Based on Daily Changes in Dow Jones Average 1989–1992**

Percent Change Over	Estimated Proportion	Actual Proportion
-8.8	96	97
-6.9	95	96
-3.6	87	87
0	60	52
3.6	21	13
6.9	6	2
8.8	3	1

Note that in the second test we worked backward, using daily changes not to predict subsequent daily changes but rather to estimate prior *annual* changes in an *entirely different* market average.

Tables 7.1 and 7.2 show proportions predicted by the method together with the actual proportions.

Careful study of this data reveals a close correspondence between predicted and actual frequencies. It is remarkable that we were able to predict annual frequencies on one series from daily data on another series; that we were able to predict frequencies over the course of more than a century from data of four years; and that (as shown in Chapter 5) we were able to predict changes over 250 trading days from the data of a single trading day. This ability to predict from such disparate samples suggests that there are some inherent characteristics that can be used to estimate the probabilities of future changes in such series as stock prices and other financial variables.

Summary

The importance of this demonstration is that we can use a short sequence of data to predict a long sequence. For example, even though we may not have enough data to determine, say, the distribution of five-year changes in the market, we will probably not be too far off if we take estimates of the distribution of monthly changes and then, using the square root rule and the normal distribution, estimate the five-year distribution. In other words, we can use short-term changes in the market to estimate the distribution of long-term changes.

In short, this demonstration suggests that the market is, in Mandelbrot's words, statistically self-similar to a remarkable degree.

CHAPTER 8

How to Reduce Common Stock Portfolio Risk

The risk in a portfolio of common stocks may be reduced by increasing the number of stocks in the portfolio and placing an equal investment in each stock. Doing this can reduce the risk of the portfolio by one-half. Further reduction in risk is not possible if the portfolio is restricted to common stocks. The reduction in risk assumes that the stocks in the portfolio have no common influences, apart from that of the market itself. If there are common influences, such as might arise if the stocks are in the same industry, then the degree of reduction in risk will be diminished. Attention to industry diversification can sharply curtail industry risk.

The mathematics of risk reduction were first presented formally by Markowitz, though the idea is common to basic statistical theory. If we take out the market effect on changes in common stock prices, we are left with a residual price change. That residual price change may be considered a random variable.

The standard deviation is a good measure of risk. By definition, the standard deviation of the average of a sum of random variables is that average divided by the square root of the number of components. The equation of the relationship is the following, where n is the number of stocks in the average:

$$\text{Standard Deviation of Average} = \text{Standard Deviation} / n^{0.5}$$

Using this equation, we can actually state the reduction in the standard deviation achieved by increasing the number of stocks (see Table 8.1).

The theoretical reduction in the residual risk of the portfolio is shown in the right-hand column, which is $1/n^{.5}$. The effect of adding stocks to the portfolio has several interesting features:

1. The second stock provides the greatest reduction in risk.

Table 8.1   Reduction in Residual Risk as the Number of Stocks Rises

Number of Stocks n	Reduction in Residual Risk $1/n^{0.5}$
1	1.00
2	.70
3	.57
4	.50
5	.45
10	.31
15	.26
20	.22
30	.18
50	.14
100	.10
1,000	.03

---

2.   Each additional stock provides less reduction in risk than its predecessor.

3.   By the time we add the ninth stock, we have reduced residual risk to one-third the original risk.

4.   To cut risk to one-tenth the original, 100 stocks are needed in the portfolio.

The practical impact of the theoretical effect is that additional stocks can have a dramatic effect on portfolio risk reduction. We can compare the theoretical reduction in risk to actual reduction by looking at the effect of portfolios created by randomly picking various numbers of stocks and placing an equal investment in each. Since the return is a single-period return, the market has no effect and we have a perfect test of the data in Table 8.1.

For that comparison, we will use data from the Fisher Lorie study of all New York Stock Exchange stocks 1945–1965. The results for two 10-year holding periods are shown in Table 8.2.

A quite remarkable correspondence exists between the expected and actual reductions in risk. The results for the period 1926–1945 (not shown) are not at all as close; I suspect the reason is that the much smaller sample available for the earlier period curtailed the reduction in risk.

Table 8.2 neglects the effect of the market on risk. Market risk, fluctuations in the Dow Jones Average or the Standard & Poor's 500, account for about half the risk in a portfolio. It is not possible to eliminate this risk. We can make a simple study of risk by examining what happens to the standard deviation of a portfolio when both the number of stocks and market risk are considered simultaneously. Table 8.3 simulates this effect.

In Table 8.3, the total standard deviation is assumed to be equal to the sum of the market standard deviation and the stock standard deviation. To be precise, the total portfo-

Table 8.2   Expected and Actual Reduction in Standard Deviation with Increase in Number of Stocks

Number of Stocks	Standard Deviation of Wealth Ratios	Expected Reduction in Standard Deviation	Actual Reduction in Standard Deviation
1	2.571	100	100
2	1.820	71	71
8	.917	35	36
16	.653	25	25
32	.469	18	18
128	.256	9	10

Table 8.3   Market, Stock, and Total Standard Deviation for Portfolios of Various Numbers of Stocks

Number of Stocks	Market Standard Deviation	Individual Stock Standard Deviation	Total Standard Deviation
1	50	50	100
2	50	35	85
3	50	29	79
4	50	25	75
5	50	22	72
6	50	20	70
7	50	19	69
8	50	18	68
9	50	17	67
10	50	16	66
16	50	13	63
32	50	9	59
128	50	4	54
inf	50	0	50

lio variance (s_p^2) is equal to the sum of the market variance (s_m^2) and the stock variance (s_s^2), as shown in Equation (8.1).

$$s_p^2 = s_m^2 + s_s^2/n \tag{8.1}$$

$$s_p = (s_m^2 + s_s^2/n)^{0.5} \tag{8.2}$$

The theoretical relationship (given in Equation 8.2, Table 8.3, and column 3 of Table 8.4) can be compared with the actual reduction shown in column 4 of Table 8.4. Table 8.4 is based on the standard deviation reported in the Fisher Lorie study, reductions for the one-year returns for the total sample over the 1926–65 period.

Clearly, there is a fairly good correspondence between the expected reduction in the standard deviation achieved by increasing the number of stocks and the actual reduction.

A later study by Evans and Archer, covering Standard & Poor's 500 stocks between January 1958 and July 1959, reveals similar results. Their findings, together with the expected results, are shown in Table 8.5.

Evans and Archer restricted their sample portfolios to a maximum of 40 stocks. Though they did not give the actual results, they did give the formula, from which we have calculated the standard deviation. As shown in Table 8.2, the expected and actual reductions in the standard deviations are fairly close.

Table 8.4   Effect of Increasing the Number of Stocks on the Standard Deviation of Portfolios (Fisher Lorie Study)

Number of Stocks	Standard Deviation of Wealth Ratios	Expected Reduction in Standard Deviation	Actual Reduction in Standard Deviation
1	.554	100	100
2	.451	85	81
8	.354	68	64
16	.335	63	60
32	.325	59	58

Table 8.5   Effect of Increasing the Number of Stocks on the Standard Deviation of Portfolios (Evans Archer Study)

Number of Stocks	Standard Deviation Annualized from Formula	Expected Reduction in Standard Deviation	Actual Reduction in Standard Deviation
1	.290	100	100
2	.229	85	79
8	.184	68	63
16	.177	63	61
32	.172	59	59
40	.171	58	59

Summary

When you invest in stocks, you can cut your risk by diversifying—by adding more stocks to your portfolio and placing an equal investment in each stock. The major reductions in risk come from adding the first few stocks. After 10 or 15 stocks, the degree of reduction achieved by adding more stocks declines. The main objective is to add stocks and thereby achieve some diversification—and thereby cut your risk.

CHAPTER 9

Are There Changes in Stock Market Volatility?

Our ability to predict stock market risk assumes that the volatility of the market doesn't change from one historical period to the next. If the volatility of the market is comparatively stable (say within a factor of two) then we can use past measures of the standard deviation to predict future measures. If this is not the case, then we cannot make as good a prediction about future volatility. Consequently, the question as to whether the variability of the market is stable is critical to prediction.

As we have seen, the level of the market must be taken into account when measuring volatility and when estimating the standard deviation. In recent markets where the Dow Jones Industrial Average exceeded 3,000, daily changes of 30, or even 50, were not unusual. When the market was 600, a daily change of that magnitude would have been extraordinary. Dollar changes in the market depend on the level of the market because the distribution of changes is lognormal. Percentage changes, or log changes, on the other hand, will not be affected by the level of the market. By measuring the standard deviation using percentage changes, or first differences in the logs, we provide a measure that is not arbitrarily affected by the level of the market.

Even a cursory glance at a chart of the stock market over a long period suggests that the volatility of the market does change. For our purpose, the real questions are the magnitude and frequency of the changes.

The first person to study changes in volatility was R.R. Officer. He examined the standard deviation of monthly returns of the Dow Jones Industrial Average from 1897 to 1969. During this period, the standard deviation was generally above 5 percent and rarely exceeded 16 percent, except during the stock market crash of 1929, when it reached twice that figure. Thus, there was a fair degree of stability to the risk in the market, with the notable exception of the period surrounding October 1929.

Table 9.1 shows the standard deviation of monthly changes in the Standard & Poor's 500 Stock Price Index over the period 1872–1991. These tables show the standard devia-

Table 9.1	Standard Deviation of Changes in Log of Standard & Poor's 500 Common Stock Index 1872–1991 (x 100)	

Years	Standard Deviation (x 100)
1872–1881	3.2
1882–1891	3.4
1892–1901	3.6
1902–1911	4.8
1912–1921	3.4
1922–1931	5.7
1932–1941	7.9
1942–1951	3.5
1952–1961	2.8
1962–1971	3.3
1972–1981	3.8
1982–1991	3.7

tion of first differences in the logs of the market index (x100). There is variation in the standard deviation, but it is relatively limited, ranging between 2.8 and 7.9, or within a factor of 3. Two-thirds of the time the range is between 3.0 and 4.0, a much smaller range than suggested by the extreme values. The log first differences (x100) approximate percentage changes, so that a monthly log change (x100) of 3.0 in Table 9.1 is approximately 3 percent.

As Table 9.1 reveals, the market volatility is certainly not invariant: The standard deviation does change from one period to the next. But the shifts in variability seem to have limits. The standard deviation appears to remain within a factor of roughly 2. Our measures of volatility appear to be sufficiently constant to allow estimation of future standard deviations, recognizing, of course, that, during occasional periods, volatility will be much higher than the past average would suggest. Overall, the standard deviation is sufficiently stable to permit reasonable estimation of future volatility.

CHAPTER 10

Predicting Probable Returns from a Single Stock

Suppose you want to know your expected return if you invest in a certain stock. You cannot know your exact return, but you can determine the range of probable returns.

To make a probability estimate of returns from buying a single stock is not difficult. You need to know three things. First, you need to know the standard deviation of past changes in the price of the stock. Then, you must know the time interval over which the probability estimate is to be made. Finally, you need the mean expected change, which we will assume to be zero. With this data, and the Probability Tables given in Appendix II, you can find the probability of any degree of change.

The steps are as follows:

1. Secure prices for a series of equally spaced intervals.

2. Compute percentage changes in the price of the stock over such intervals.

3. Calculate the standard deviation of the percentage price changes.

4. Multiply the standard deviation by one of the following factors in order to derive the one-year standard deviation:

Original Data	Factor
Weekly prices	7.2x
Monthly prices	3.5x
Annual prices	1.0x

5. Look up the probability of changes in the Probability Tables (see Appendix II).

Table 10.1 provides an example of changes in the price and a calculation of the standard deviation. In this example, the standard deviation of the percentage changes in price is 38 percent. We don't need to multiply the standard deviation by the appropriate factor, since we have annual changes.

Next, turn to the Probability Tables (in Appendix II). Rounding off 38 percent, we will use the column labeled 40 percent. The data in Table 10.2 is taken from Appendix Table IIa for one-year periods for a 40 percent standard deviation.

In Table 10.2, the first column shows the percentage rise (or fall). The second column shows the probability of a rise (or fall) of at least that shown. For a rise of at least 60 percent, the probability is 8 percent. The probably of a fall of at least 40 percent is 6 percent .

Table 10.2 provides estimates of what the probabilities are. If you are interested in a longer period, say five years, use the data in Appendix II for the appropriate number of years.

Table 10.2 and Appendix II are based on the assumption that the distribution of changes in the price of a stock conforms to a lognormal distribution. The probabilities listed in Appendix II are derived from the standard deviation of changes in the logs of price but are expressed in terms of percentage changes. For log changes under 15 percent, the log change is approximately the same.

Sometimes you can obtain the standard deviation directly from another source, without calculating it yourself. In that case, provided you have an annual standard deviation, you can go directly to the Probability Table.

Summary

An estimate of probable returns from buying one stock will tell you several things. It will tell you the probability of any particular gain, like doubling your money in one year, or in 10; or increasing your investment by 10 percent in the next six months, or two years. It will also tell you the probability of losing money on the investment—losing half your investment, for example, in the next year, or in the next decade; or losing 10 percent in the next half-year. It will tell you whether the odds of a positive return are better than the flip of a coin, or not. The estimate gives you the probability of various things happening once you order the stock purchased and send your check to your broker.

The probability estimate *won't* tell you how much you will gain. The probability estimate will enable you to check assertions on odds made by someone else. If someone tells you that there is a 90 percent chance of doubling your money, the table will tell you the odds of that happening. The table won't tell you what *will* happen. It gives you the *probability* of something happening. Not a definite answer—only the probability.

Table 10.1   **Example of Finding the Standard Deviation of the Change in the Price of a Stock**

Year	Price	Percent Change
1	42	
2	49	17%
3	63	29
4	50	-21
5	27	-46
6	44	63
7	52	18
Standard Deviation		38.4%

Table 10.2   **Standard Deviation of 40% One Year in the Future**

Rise of at Least	Probability of Rise (%) $\frac{1}{n}$
200%	
150	0%
100	3
90	3
80	4
70	6
60	8
50	11
40	16
30	22
20	29
10	39
0	50

Fall of at Least	Probability of Fall
0	50
-10	30
-20	25
-30	14
-40	6
-50	2
-60	0

CHAPTER 11

Estimating Probable Returns on a Mutual Fund

Most mutual funds are appraised on the basis of their past performance record, generally over the last year, three years, five years, or decade. Mutual fund rating services usually provide these statistics and rank mutual funds on the basis of the overall record over a given interval of time. Mutual fund advertisements, which are restricted in the kind and method of presentation, provide this kind of record. But the total return over a period is not always the best measure on which to gauge the future, however appealing that may seem.

The records of most funds vary widely from one year to the next, and one decade to the next. Very few mutual funds, for example, remain in the top quartile, even the top half, for 10 years running.

The best fund is often the most volatile—the one with a good probability of really crashing when the market drops! A fund at the top of the list in an up market is often a roller coaster fund that will bounce around like a yo-yo.

Mutual funds will behave just like the market, but often will be more volatile—unless the fund is an index fund designed to mirror the Standard & Poor's 500, or another index.

To see how volatile a fund is, you can look at the standard deviation of annual returns, preferably for seven or eight years. You can also estimate the annual standard deviation from monthly data, weekly data, or daily data by multiplying the standard deviation by the appropriate factor (as shown in Chapter 10).

The annual returns on a typical mutual fund are given in Table 11.1. The returns include dividends received and the change in market value expressed as a percent of the fund value at the beginning of the year. Returns are expressed in percent.

The standard deviation of the returns of the fund illustrated in Table 11.1 is 34 percent. The method of calculating the standard deviation is given in Chapter 2.

To get the probabilities of future returns, use Appendix II, Table IIa. In that table, look up the column under the standard deviation of 35 percent for one year in the future. The

35 percent is close enough to the 34 percent actual. For illustration, part of Table IIa has been reproduced in Table 11.2.

The table shows the probabilities of gain or loss for a mutual fund with a standard deviation of 35 percent. There is a 50 percent probability the fund will rise—and an equal probability that it will fall. There is a 1 percent probability that it will rise by 100 percent, or double in value, and an equal, or 1 percent probability, that it will halve, or fall by 50

Table 11.1   Example of Annual Returns on a Mutual Fund

Year	Annual Return (%)
1	+80
2	+15
3	+10
4	-25
5	+ 5
6	-20
7	+17

Table 11.2   Standard Deviation 35% One Year in Future

Increase of at Least	Probability (%)
100%	1%
90	2
80	3
70	4
60	6
50	9
40	13
30	19
20	27
10	38
0	50

Decrease of at Least	Probability (%)
0	50
-10	36
-20	23
-30	12
-40	4
-50	1

percent. That gives you some idea of the risk. The chance of a 30 percent fall is 12 percent, or 1 in 8. The tables are based on the assumption that the returns have a lognormal distribution.

Table 11.2 gives probable returns for one year in the future. For longer periods you have to use one of the other tables in Appendix II. There are tables for 1, 2, 3, 4, 5, 10, and 15 years. For longer periods, you can also multiply the standard deviation by the square root of the number of years to produce a new standard deviation. Find the appropriate column for the new standard deviation; then look up the probabilities as before to determine what your potential risks or rewards are likely to be.

Note that in the table the positive and negative probabilities are not the same. Only the log changes are equal.

CHAPTER 12

Predicting the Probability of Loss

Estimating the probability of loss is similar to finding the probable changes in the price of a stock, the probable future returns on a fund, or the probable changes in profit margins. But there is a slight twist to the matter that alters the computation.

To find the probability of loss, we look at the probability distribution of future changes in profits in relation to how far they currently are above or below zero profits. We measure the distance above or below zero profits in terms of the number of standard deviations of past changes in profits. We then can apply the normal distribution to find the probability of a change in profits large enough to reduce profits to zero or below, or to keep profits below zero.

Loss, in the sense used here, means negative profits, or the failure of a company to earn a profit. Profits are defined as reported earnings after deduction of amortization and depreciation charges but before noncurrent items, such as extraordinary write-offs. This definition is not essential to the method described here, for the same method may be applied to other definitions of profit and loss, cash flow, profit margins, or other variables. The same methodology is applicable to various measures of profit and loss.

To find the probability of loss, take the following steps.

1. Collect seven or more years of earnings data.

2. Compute annual changes in earnings.

3. Find the standard deviation of past changes in earnings.

4. Divide the most recent annual earnings figure by the standard deviation of past changes in earnings to obtain the *z-score*. The z-score is a statistical term applied to a value divided by the standard deviation of changes in that value so that it can be used easily with the normal distribution.

**Table 12.1   Example of Earnings Per Share and
Change in Earnings Per Share of a Company**

Year	Earnings	Change in Earnings
1	1.21	
2	1.80	+0.59
3	0.75	-1.05
4	0.05	-0.70
5	0.57	+0.52
6	0.40	-0.17
7	0.15	-0.25

---

5.   From the *Probability of Loss* table (Table 12.3 or Appendix V), find the probability of loss.

If profits are positive, use the part of Table 12.2 for positive profit. If profits are negative, use the part of Table 12.3 for negative profits. This procedure gives you the probability of a loss in the forthcoming year.

Let's take an example.

1.   Collect seven or more years of earnings data, as shown in Table 12.1.

2.   Compute annual changes in earnings (as in Table 12.1).

3.   Find the standard deviation of changes.

$$\text{Standard Deviation} = 0.65$$

4.   Determine how many standard deviations above, or below, zero earnings the most recent earnings figure is by dividing the latest profit figure by the standard deviation.

We divide the latest earnings figure, $0.15, by the standard deviation, 0.65, giving 0.23. This is the z-score defined as a quantity divided by its standard deviation.

$$\text{z–score} = 0.15 / 0.65$$
$$= 0.23$$

5.   From the table of the Probability of Loss, find the probability for a company whose earnings are positive. Table 12.2 shows that for a z-score of 0.25 the probability of loss is 40 percent. For a z-score of 0.20 the probability is 42 percent. So the probability of loss is between these two figures, or about 41 percent.

$$\text{Probability of Loss} = 41\%$$

Table 12.2　Table for Finding Probability of Loss—Positive Earnings

Earnings/Standard Deviation of Earnings (z-score)	Probability of Loss (%)
.00	50%
.05	48
.10	46
.15	44
.20	42
.25	40
.30	38
.35	36
.40	34
.50	31
.60	27
.70	24
.80	21
.90	18

6.　If profits are negative, use the portion of Table 12.3 for negative profits. In making the computation, we used reported earnings per share. The same kind of computation could have been applied using another measure of profits, such as actual profits in millions of dollars, profit margins, return on total assets, or even percentage changes in profits.

It's best normally to use reported profits in per share figures or total dollars, as we did in this example. But if there are large shifts in profits, as might occur from a merger, then use an alternative measure, such as return on assets, or profit margins. Use the alternative measure of profits just as we used the earnings per share figures above. If you are using profit margins, find the change in margins each year; compute the standard deviation of changes in margins; and finally divide the latest margin by the standard deviation to obtain the z-score. Then look up the z-score in the table.

Use of profit margins, return on total assets, or return on equity provides a figure that is not affected by arbitrary accounting changes, such as those that might result from a merger or acquisition. In a long study of the probability of loss, we used earnings/assets in order to obtain comparable figures for a large group of companies. This transformation homogenized the data and made year-to-year changes more comparable.

What is needed in assessing the probability of loss is a measure of the variability of earnings and then a measure of how far profits are above or below zero by the latest figure. The latest figure is generally the best measure of future profits. By standardizing that figure as a z-score (by dividing it by the standard deviation of changes), we can apply the normal curve to estimate the probability of loss. We can also make forecasts of the probability of loss in future years by multiplying the standard deviation by the square root of the number of years after completing Step 2. Then proceed as before, and you have your answer.

The probability of loss that you derive by the this method has a number of significant advantages over other measures. The probability for one company will be strictly comparable with that of another, irrespective of what industry each company happens to be in. The measure is not affected by arbitrary scaling of the variables as are other measures of credit risk, like Altman's z-score. Loss is a good indicator of future problems, such as nonpayment of interest or principal on a loan, reduction in the dividend, and even bankruptcy.

If the future performance of a company is of concern, it is helpful to compute the probability of loss using the method in this chapter.

Table 12.3   Table for Finding Probability of Loss

POSITIVE EARNINGS

Earnings/Standard Deviation of Changes in Earnings (z-score)	Probability of Loss (%)
.00	50%
.05	48
.10	46
.15	44
.20	42
.25	40
.30	38
.35	36
.40	34
.50	31
.60	27
.70	24
.80	21
.90	18
1.00	16
1.10	14
1.20	11
1.30	10
1.40	8
1.50	7
1.60	6
1.70	5

(Table 12.3 continues)

(Table 12.3 continued)

Earnings/Standard Deviation of Changes in Earnings (z-score)	Probability of Loss (%)
1.80	4
1.90	3
2.00	2
2.25	1

NEGATIVE EARNINGS

Earnings/Standard Deviation of Changes in Earnings (z-score)	Probability of Loss (%)
.00	50%
.05	52
.10	54
.15	56
.20	58
.25	60
.30	62
.35	64
.40	66
.50	69
.60	73
.70	76
.80	79
.90	82
1.00	84
1.10	86
1.20	88
1.30	90
1.40	92
1.50	93
1.60	95
1.70	96
1.80	96
1.90	97
2.00	98
2.25	99

CHAPTER 13

Predicting Probable Changes in Earnings

A Scenario

I'll never forget that year. It was the year of little snow, a year in which the ice boaters took their vacations in January so they could spend their days racing across the clear, frozen stretches of Lake Minnetonka. It was also a year when companies that made snow-plowing equipment reeled, as if hit by the plague, for the dry winter crucified revenues and sent earnings below zero.

Harry Sutch had come to see me the previous summer. Harry was the most unanalytical-looking securities analyst I'd ever met: short and heavyset, with thick eyebrows over sleepy eyes, always dressed in a rumpled, tweedy sport coat that never matched his slacks. Harry's disheveled appearance was misleading, for his mind was quick and precise. Harry always could get to the bottom of things, and he never quit until he had.

Harry's visit to me was just an early stop on his route, investigating one company or another. As he slouched into the nearest leather chair, he explained that the *Farmer's Almanac* predicted a dry winter coming up and he wondered how it might affect snow-blower companies. If they got hit by a snow drought, it would drive their earnings underground.

I knew the bad earnings wouldn't hit the papers for a year; the drop would take place in the March quarter, which would be reported in June, since it takes about three months for the figures to be reported. If the *Farmer's Almanac* proved right, the snow-blower industry would have trouble. The question was, how much trouble? How far would earnings drop?

"That's why I came to you," Harry said. "I remembered you'd figured out how to estimate the volatility of earnings and their levels for various probabilities. I want to know what the downside risk is."

I then explained how to make the estimate: gather seven or eight years of earnings data. Then get your calculator and calculate the percentage change from year to year so you've got six or seven changes in earnings per share.

Then I laid out the data (as shown in Table 13.1). The second column gives earnings per share. The third column gives the percentage change in earnings per share.

Next, I computed the standard deviation of the right-hand column, the annual percentage changes in earnings. I worked it out with a calculator that could compute the standard deviation. The standard deviation turned out to be 20 percent.

Then I turned to a table showing the probabilities of various percentage changes for that standard deviation.

The relevant data from the table (Appendix II, Table IIa in this book) are given in Table 13.2. The numbers in the right-hand column are the probabilities.

There is an 11 percent chance of at least a 20 percent fall in earnings and a 3 percent chance of at least a 30 percent drop in earnings.

Harry noted that, if the 3 percent chance of a 30 percent fall occurred, there would be serious problems. And if the snow stayed away next winter, the 3 percent would underestimate the odds.

Harry's expression combined satisfaction and grimness.

"I know now what the odds are," he said at last. "That helps a lot. It gives me a solid estimate of the probabilities—which is just what I needed."

Table 13.1   Earnings Per Share and Percent Changes in Earnings

Year	Earnings Per Share	Percent Change
1	0.86	
2	0.92	+ 7
3	1.13	+23
4	1.02	-10
5	1.25	+23
6	0.97	-22
7	1.20	+24

Table 13.2   20% Standard Deviation One Year in Future

Fall of at Least	Probability
0%	50%
-5	39
-10	28
-20	11
-30	3
-40	-

Predicting Changes in Earnings

Earnings are perhaps the most important variable affecting a corporation, whether they be in the form of the stock price, the payment of dividends, the payment of interest and repayment of principal, or, in the end, the very continuance of the organization and its provision of goods and services to customers and employment to its employees. For these reasons, earnings are very important.

In attempting to evaluate the corporation, it is important to be able to make some kind of statement about future earnings. That, of course, means forecasting the range of probable changes in earnings.

The procedure described above is the same procedure we use in forecasting changes in other variables, like stock prices or the future probable returns on a mutual fund. It involves the following steps:

1. Obtain a series of earnings figures for the past seven or more years.

2. Compute annual changes in earnings. You can use percentage changes, provided that none of the earnings figures is zero or negative. You can also use changes in the logs, though that may not be necessary.

3. Calculate the standard deviation of the changes in earnings.

    If some of the earnings figures are negative you can use the actual figures to calculate the standard deviation and then express the resulting standard deviation as a percent of the latest earnings figure.

4. Look up the probable changes in the Table of Probability, given in Appendix II.

CHAPTER 14

Predicting Probable Changes in Profit Margins

A Scenario

Some people are born optimists. They always look at the positive side of things, sure that whatever they do—or buy—will turn out well. Bob was such a person. He was forever optimistic about life in general, but particularly about the industry in which he had spent his life's work—the television industry.

His rosy view of the future of the prices of television stations was typical. When television stations were selling at 10 times operating cash flow, Bob was sure the price would rise to 12 times operating cash flow. When station prices rose to 12 times, he was certain the next price would be 14 times operating cash flow.

"The prices," he liked to say, "reflect the inevitable growth of the television industry. Ad revenues rose with inflation, only at a faster rate. An annual 10 percent rise in operating margins was foreordained. The more likely figure will be 20 percent."

His firm belief in these matters was an article of faith. He had seen it happen for two decades. He saw no reason, therefore, for the growth not to continue.

Bob and I had a mutual friend who was a director of a television station. The friend came to me one day with a question that related to Bob's optimistic view of the industry.

"We're looking at acquiring a new television station in a regional city," he said. "Bob is very much for it. But I'm concerned that we can't afford to make the purchase."

"What's the problem?" I asked.

"The buyer wants a high price for the station. We don't know what the asking price is, but we think it's on the order of $18 million. We also figured we'd have to bid that high to beat three other bidders."

"Eighteen million," I repeated. "That is high."

"It is," he continued, "though how high depends on what the television station is earning."

"What is it earning?"

"The relevant figure is the price to operating cash flow. A price of $18 million is 20 times projected operating cash flow."

"That's much higher than the usual 12 or 14 times," I said.

"Exactly," he replied. "The only way we can make the deal work—particularly, factoring in the interest costs on the debt we'd have to take on—is to raise margins."

"Raise them how much?"

"Substantially. From 27 percent to 35 percent."

"How can you do it?"

"Well, Bob says the industry average is 35 percent. This station's margins at 27 percent are well below the industry. Bob thinks that by cutting unnecessary costs, we should not have a difficult time bringing the station up to the industry average."

He paused for a moment, and then continued.

"That's why I wanted to see you. I want to know what you think the likelihood is of raising margins from 27 percent to 35 percent."

"The first thing to do," I said, "is to look at past margins, see what they look like, and see how changeable they are."

The margins he showed me are given in Table 14.1.

"Now," I said, "to get some idea of how probable it is that margins can be raised from the latest figure of 27 percent to 35 percent, look at how much margins have changed in the past.

"Begin by putting down annual changes in margins (shown in the right-hand column). Then look at the magnitude of past changes. If they are all much lower than the 8 percent change, then there isn't much chance of making that big a change. But if past changes are 8 percent or more, then there might be a good chance."

"You can actually calculate the probability of reaching a margin of 35 percent from the data. First, see how many standard deviations are involved in the change from 28 percent to 35 percent. Then look up the probability of getting that many standard deviations from a table of the normal probability curve."

I continued, "Let's first find the standard deviation." I did the calculation on my calculator and came up with a figure of approximately 7 percent.

"Here's what we do."

Then I went over the steps:

Table 14.1   Profit Margins and Changes in Profit Margins

Year	Profit Margin (%)	Change in Profit Margin
1	25	
2	27	+ 2
3	19	- 8
4	22	+ 3
5	29	+ 7
6	21	- 8
7	27	+ 6

1. Find the amount of change required to go from 27 percent to 35 percent. We've done that already. It's 8 percent.

2. Compute the standard deviation of past changes. That's the standard deviation of those changes in the right-hand column of Table 14.1.

Standard Deviation of Changes in Margins = 7%

3. Divide the required change, the 8 percent, by the standard deviation of past changes, or by 7 percent.

Change in Margins / Standard Deviation = 8 / 7

= 1.14

= z–score

"So, to hit the 35 percent margin, margins have to increase 1.14 standard deviations," he said.

"That's right," I replied.

"What, then, is the probability of moving 1.14 standard deviations?" my friend asked.

"You can look it up in a table of the normal curve." (See Table 14.2.)

The z-score of 1.14 lies between 1.10 and 1.20. The corresponding probabilities are 14 percent and 11 percent. The probability of raising margins by 8 percent was therefore 12 to 13 percent.

My friend looked a little worried.

"Though Bob will think that's easy," he said with a trace of concern in his voice, "I don't think it will be. After all, margins can go down as well as up. And they've never been at 35 percent before."

I nodded in agreement. He had an objective estimate of what the probability was of improving margins by that amount. The numbers were not that reassuring.

"It's possible," I agreed. "but not easy."

The method explained in this chapter is a good way to quantify a possibility. It can be used whenever you want to know what the odds are of improving margins by a given amount.

Table 14.2   Table for Finding Probability of Change in Margins

Change in Margin/Standard Deviation of Change (z-scores)	Probability of Change (%)
.00	50%
.05	48
.10	46
.15	44
.20	42
.25	40
.30	38
.35	36
.40	34
.50	31
.60	27
.70	24
.80	21
.90	18
1.00	16
1.10	14
1.20	11
1.30	10
1.40	8
1.50	7
1.60	6
1.70	5
1.80	4
1.90	3
2.00	2
2.25	1

CHAPTER 15

How to Estimate the Average Future Return from Stocks

What will the future return from stocks be? The fact is, we don't know precisely, and whatever estimate we make will most likely be wrong. Yet it is essential to make some kind of estimate of the long-run return of the stock market. What's the right way to do it, and what's the wrong way? Unfortunately, one misleading way is very prevalent today, as will be explained in this chapter.

There are two principal methods of estimating the long-run average return on a stock portfolio. One method is to estimate the mean from past returns. The second is to calculate it from the cross-section standard deviation. Each method has advantages and disadvantages.

The second method is the easiest. But it presumes we know the cross-section standard deviation of changes in the logs of stock prices. The distribution of changes in the logs of stock prices is a normal distribution. When we calculate returns on stock prices, we calculate them from the prices themselves, not from the logs. When you have a (continuous) distribution whose logs are normal, the mean of the antilogs is given by the exponent of one-half the squared standard deviation, or

$$\text{Mean } = \text{ exp (Average } + \text{ Standard Deviation}^2 / 2) \qquad (15.1)$$

If we assume the average is zero, then the equation becomes

$$\text{Mean } = \text{ exp (Standard Deviation}^2 / 2) \qquad (15.2)$$

where the standard deviation is computed as the difference in the logs of prices across stocks, or as the cross-sectional standard deviation.

Based on Equation (15.2), mean changes in the market for various standard deviations (assuming the mean change in the log is zero) are as shown in Table 15.1.

When the standard deviation is 0.30, the expected mean change is 4.6 percent per year.

When the cross-sectional standard deviation of annual changes in the logs of prices is 0.35, the mean is 6.3 percent. If we estimate the mean annual cross-sectional standard deviation from the Fisher Lorie data (see Chapter 16) on all New York Stock Exchange common stocks from 1926 to 1965, we obtain 0.28, which results in a mean annual price rise of 4.6 percent.

The above calculations assume a mean change of zero in the logs of prices. If there is a mean change, use Equation (15.1). If you use the 0.30 figure above, which seem reasonable, you obtain a rounded figure of about 5 percent per year. Add the dividend, and your total return works out to be more like 8 percent. That's one good approach to finding the expected long-run return from the stock market.

Over the long run, the returns on a return of 4.6 percent can be remarkable. One thousand dollars invested at 4.6 percent at the time the Declaration of Independence was signed would be worth $17,313,128 by 1993.

Estimating the Mean Growth in the Market from the Cross-Sectional Standard Deviation —An Illustration

We can illustrate how to estimate the future return from the market using Equation (15.2) above.

Table 15.2 shows the cross-section interquartile range of annual total returns of all New York Stock Exchange stocks for each year from 1926 to 1989 and statistics that can be derived from that data. The cross-sectional data was prepared by R. W. McEnally and R. B. Todd. Columns 2 and 3 give the total returns for the first and third quartiles. One-fourth of all stocks have returns less than the first quartile; similarly, one-fourth have

Table 15.1   Estimates of the Annual Mean Change in the Stock Market from Various Standard Deviations of the Mean Change in the Natural Logarithms

Standard Deviation	Mean Change
.10	0.5%
.15	1.1
.20	2.0
.25	3.2
.30	4.6
.35	6.3
.40	8.3
.45	10.7
.50	13.3

Table 15.2	Estimating the Mean Growth in the Market from the Cross-Sectional Standard Deviation Based on NYSE 1st and 3rd Quartile Annual Total Returns, 1926–1989*						
	% Change Quartile		Log Change Quartile		Inter Quartile Range	Std. Dev.	Annual Growth Percent
Year	1st	3rd	1st	3rd			
(1)	(2)	(3)	(4)	(5)	(6)	(7)	(8)
1926	-19	18	-.21	.16	.37	.28	3.9
1927	0	54	0	.43	.43	.32	5.2
1928	3	65	.03	.50	.47	.35	6.4
1929	-54	-5	-.77	-.05	.72	.54	15.4
1930	-58	-19	-.87	-.21	.66	.49	12.8
1931	-67	-32	-1.10	-.38	.71	.53	15.0
1932	-37	11	-.46	.10	.57	.42	9.3
1933	34	163	.30	.97	.67	.50	13.2
1934	-17	37	-.19	.31	.50	.37	7.1
1935	11	80	.10	.59	.49	.36	6.7
1936	12	69	.11	.52	.41	.31	4.8
1937	-60	-34	-.92	-.42	.50	.37	7.0
1938	7	54	.07	.43	.36	.27	3.7
1939	-25	15	-.28	.14	.42	.31	4.9
1940	-22	4	-.25	.04	.30	.22	2.4
1941	-29	6	-.34	.06	.39	.29	4.4
1942	3	47	.03	.38	.35	.26	3.4
1943	24	73	.21	.55	.33	.25	6.1
1944	19	51	.17	.41	.24	.18	1.6
1945	35	75	.30	.56	.26	.19	1.9
1946	-26	5	-.30	.05	.35	.26	6.4
1947	-17	14	-.18	.13	.31	.23	2.7
1948	-16	9	-.17	.09	.26	.19	1.8
1949	4	35	.04	.30	.26	.20	1.9
1950	10	56	.09	.45	.35	.26	3.5
1951	2	27	.02	.24	.22	.16	1.3
1952	-4	23	-.04	.20	.24	.18	1.7
1953	-16	7	-.17	.07	.24	.18	1.6
1954	31	75	.27	.56	.29	.22	2.4
1955	4	31	.04	.27	.23	.17	1.5
1956	-8	20	-.08	.18	.27	.20	2.0
1957	-31	4	-.36	.04	.40	.30	4.5

(Table 15.2 continues)

Year	% Change Quartile		Log Change Quartile		Inter Quartile Range	Std. Dev.	Annual Growth Percent
	1st	3rd	1st	3rd			
(1)	(2)	(3)	(4)	(5)	(6)	(7)	(8)
1958	35	72	.30	.54	.24	.18	1.7
1959	-3	27	-.03	.24	.27	.20	2.0
1960	-21	15	-.23	.14	.37	.28	3.9
1961	9	43	.08	.35	.27	.20	2.0
1962	-26	0	-.31	0	.31	.23	2.6
1963	3	31	.03	.27	.24	.18	1.6
1964	3	30	.03	.26	.23	.17	1.5
1965	4	46	.04	.38	.34	.25	3.2
1966	-22	2	-.25	.02	.27	.20	2.1
1967	14	71	.13	.54	.41	.30	4.6
1968	6	44	.06	.36	.31	.23	2.6
1969	-37	-6	-.47	-.06	.40	.30	4.6
1970	-22	14	-.25	.13	.38	.28	4.1
1971	-2	34	-.02	.29	.31	.23	2.8
1972	-9	24	-.09	.21	.30	.23	2.6
1973	-48	-12	-.66	-.13	.53	.40	8.1
1974	-43	-13	-.56	-.13	.43	.32	5.2
1975	23	84	.20	.61	.41	.30	4.6
1976	20	61	.18	.48	.29	.22	2.4
1977	-9	20	-.09	.18	.27	.20	2.1
1978	-6	22	-.07	.20	.27	.20	2.0
1979	5	53	.05	.43	.38	.28	4.0
1980	1	48	.01	.39	.38	.28	4.0
1981	-18	24	-.19	.22	.41	.31	4.8
1982	0	50	0	.41	.40	.30	4.6
1983	9	47	.09	.39	.30	.22	2.5
1984	-19	17	-.21	.16	.37	.27	3.8
1985	9	46	.08	.38	.30	.22	2.5
1986	-7	31	-.07	.27	.34	.25	3.3
1987	-23	12	-.27	.12	.38	.28	4.1
1988	2	33	.02	.29	.26	.20	1.9
1989	-5	39	-.05	.33	.38	.28	4.1
Average						.271	3.7
in Percent						31.1	

returns greater than the fourth quartile. Thus, between the first and third quartile figures (columns 2 and 3), lie half the total returns.

We can convert the quartile percentage changes to log changes, which we can then use to make further estimates. Log changes are distributed more normally than percentage changes. Columns 4 and 5 give the results of converting the percentage returns in columns 2 and 3 to log changes. For percentages between -10 percent and +10 percent, the log changes are very close to the percentage changes (after dividing the percentages by 100).

We need the interquartile range to calculate the standard deviation. Column 6 gives the interquartile range, the difference between columns 4 and 5. The interquartile range varies from a low of 0.22 to a high of 0.72. The high is 3.3 times the low, a much lower difference than that between the high and low percentage changes where the high is 5.3 times the low.

Once we have the interquartile range, we can compute the standard deviation. For a normally distributed population, the interquartile range represents 1.349 standard deviations. Since rates of return on stocks form an approximately normal distribution, we can divide the interquartile range by 1.349 to obtain an estimate of the standard deviation. Column 7 gives the standard deviations estimated by dividing the corresponding interquartile ranges in column 6 by 1.349.

We now can substitute our estimate of the cross-sectional standard deviation, s, in the formula $\exp(s^2/2)$ to obtain an estimate of the mean growth in the market. When the standard deviation is 0.30, Equation (15.2) gives

$$\exp(.30^2/2)$$
$$= \exp(.09/2)$$
$$= \exp(.045)$$
$$= 1.046$$

The value 1.046 is that obtained at the end of one year on an investment of $1.00 made at the beginning of the year, representing an annual compound growth of 4.6 percent. Column 8 lists the annual percentage growth rates that we estimated from the annual cross-sectional standard deviations.

In the table, we show data to two places; in making the calculations for each column, however, we used more places. Consequently, what is shown in columns 4 to 8 may be slightly different from what you might calculate from the rounded data given in columns 2 and 3.

The mean standard deviation, as estimated from the interquartile range, is 0.271, or 31.1 percent. The estimated annual growth, based on that standard deviation, is 4.2 percent. That figure is not far from actual growth of the market. Our interquartile ranges were computed from total returns, not from capital appreciation returns only. The latter figure would have been preferable, but was not available.

The above estimates of growth of the market are based on a normal distribution of changes in the logs of prices of individual stocks. When that is the case (as it is to an approximate degree), the price changes themselves will be skewed, so positive percentage changes will tend to exceed negative percentage changes. Positive and negative log changes will tend to exceed negative percentage changes. Positive and negative log changes, however, will be of the same magnitude. One result of the skewing of actual price changes is that the mean price change will tend to exceed the median change. The expected change in the median will be zero; the expected change in the mean will be positive.

One of the few sources of cross-sectional data is the Fisher and Lorie study. The Fisher and Lorie annual cross-sectional data for the years 1926–1965 contains total returns with the median and mean figures. In 36 of the 40 years, the mean total return exceeded the median total return, as suggested by the model. The mean return exceeded the median return by 5.7 percent. In the absence of dividends, the median return should be positive and negative in an equal number of years; in the above sample, it was positive in 24 years and negative in 16. Since the rates of return included dividends, we would expect the median return to be greater than zero more often than not, which was the case. Without dividends, the number of positive and negative changes would be more nearly equal.

In conclusion, the mean change in the market and in a stock portfolio may be expected to be positive and to exceed the median change. The expected median change is zero. Assuming that price changes are continuous, we can estimate the mean change from the cross-sectional standard deviation using the formula: Mean Change = $\exp(s^2/2)$, where s, the cross-sectional standard deviation, is measured in logs.

We used this formula and an estimate of the standard deviation computed from inter-quartile ranges for New York Stock Exchange stocks. For the 1926–1989 sample period, the estimate of the mean change in the market was 4.2 percent. For the 1926–1965 data from Fisher and Lorie, the mean standard deviation was 32.2 percent and the estimated annual standard deviation in logarithms ranged from 0.165 to 0.551. The high was 3.3 times the low and the mean was 0.28. The estimated annual mean change in the market was 4.6 percent, as mentioned earlier.

Estimating Future Returns from Actual Changes in the Market

The second method of estimating the long-run rate of return is to look at actual changes in the market, with or without an adjustment for dividends. The important point in using this method is not to count the same evidence twice. We discussed this briefly in Chapter 1. Don't double count; that is, don't calculate the mean change several times and use some of the same data more than once.

This is a frequently made error. It's not unusual to see the same data used eight or 10 times. It's done by using overlapping intervals. While this practice is very common, it's also *very misleading*. If two centuries of effort in the statistical theory of measurement have discovered one thing, it's that you must take independent samples. Otherwise, you have a biased sample and you can't measure the probable error of your result.

Let's look at returns since 1790 (see Table 15.3) and show what to do and what not to do.

The first two columns are calculated in the same way as an actual presentation of what the market would do. The same kind of presentation is used in the well-known Ibbotson-

Table 15.3	How to Measure the Mean Change in the Stock Market		

Overlapping Periods*	Mean Return	Independent Periods	Mean Return
(1)	(2)	(3)	(4)
1980–1990	17.6	1980–1990	17.6
1970–1990	11.6	1970–1979	5.9
1960–1990	10.3	1960–1969	7.8
1950–1990	12.5	1950–1959	19.4
1940–1990	11.8	1940–1949	9.2
1930–1990	9.8	1930–1939	-0.1
1920–1990	10.2	1920–1929	12.9
1910–1990	9.4	1910–1919	4.1
1900–1990	9.4	1900–1909	9.7
1890–1990	9.1	1890–1899	5.5
1880–1990	8.7	1880–1889	5.7
1870–1980	8.7	1870–1879	8.1
1860–1990	9.2	1860–1879	15.9
1850–1990	8.6	1850–1859	1.1
1840–1990	8.7	1840–1849	9.1
1830–1990	8.3	1830–1839	2.5
1820–1990	8.2	1820–1829	6.8
1810–1990	8.2	1810–1819	9.1
1800–1990	8.3	1800–1809	9.0
1790–1990	8.4	1790–1799	10.4

Average compound annual rates.
*To the beginning of 1990.

Adapted with permission from Ibbotson, R. and Brinson, G., *Investment Markets: Gaining the Performance Advantage*, McGraw Hill, New York, 1986, Table 5.6, page 77.

independent. The periods overlap excessively; the level of the market in 1990, for example, appears in every figure. That multiple use of the same ending date biases the results. Not only that, but you can't measure the probable error using this method.

The data in columns 3 and 4 show the correct way to estimate. Look at column 3, independent periods: None of the data is overlapping. Each decade is independent. You can see that the figures in column 4 are quite different. Nine of the 20 independent decades are below 8 percent. In the overlapping sample, on the other hand, none were below 8 percent. Also, in the independent data, seven of the 20 figures are 5.9 percent or less. If you want to know the long-run behavior (assuming the behavior has not changed), you must take independent (non-overlapping) samples.

If you want to use the data in columns 1 and 2, you should use only the return for the entire period 1790–1990. That return figure is 8.4 percent. It's much better to use this figure than any of the others. If no structural changes have occurred in the market to warrant a more recent figure, then the 8.4 percent figure is the best to use.

If you are not going to use that single figure, then you should proceed as in columns 3 and 4. These contain decade returns for non-overlapping decades.

We can determine the probable error by taking the standard deviation of returns. The probable error of a mean is the standard deviation of the mean divided by the square root of the number of items.

The standard error of the mean is:

$$\text{Standard Deviation} / (n - 1)^{0.5}$$

$$= 5.1 / (20 - 1)^{0.5}$$

$$= 5.1 / 4.36$$

$$= 1.2$$

Technically, that means the decade mean should lie between 8.4 − 1.2 and 8.4 + 1.2, or between 7.2 and 9.6 two-thirds of the time. If you examine the right-hand column, you will see that is not the case. The mean was between these figures in six decades.

Summary

Use of non-overlapping decades gives us a much more reliable means of estimating the mean return from stocks than using overlapping data and thereby double counting. Look carefully at the figures if you are evaluating stocks versus bonds or looking at the record of a mutual fund when that record uses overlapping data.

CHAPTER 16

The Law of the Distribution of Wealth

The dispersion of stock prices has the inevitable consequence that some investors become increasingly wealthy while others become increasingly poor. If 100 investors begin with equal capital and each invests in a different stock, at the end of an hour, some will have slightly more than others. At the end of a day, the disparity will be even greater, by the end of a decade the disparity will be pronounced, and after a generation, some of the original 100 will be quite rich and others will have lost most of their capital. We assume, of course, that each of the 100 investors kept his money invested in the original stock.

Every stock trader and every investor probably knows or suspects that this dispersion of gains and losses from market action takes place. The dispersion is a cross-sectional dispersion, or dispersion across stocks, as some stocks rise in value and others fall. If we take out the mean change in price of all stocks, the market change, we can measure the dispersion across stocks as a function of time. The standard deviation of changes in the logs of value increases with the square root of time (described in Chapter 5).

The dispersion that characterizes the prices of stocks also characterizes market values, sales and earnings of companies, individual incomes, individual wealth—in fact, a wide range of economic variables.

Yet, coupled with this inevitable dispersion is the other apparently, but not actually, contradictory fact that each of the 100 investors in the above example has the same probability of percentage increase or decrease, irrespective of how much his or her stock has gained or lost in past years or days. If you were the lucky one and gained the most, your chance of a 10 percent gain in the next year is no greater than that of those who gained the least.

The same phenomenon also applies to corporate profits, corporate dividends, corporate assets, and corporate market values. Superior past performance does not guarantee superior future performance, or vice versa. And the same rule applies to many other economic variables, as well.

How does the process just described affect the ending value of your portfolio, or terminal wealth? In a statistical sense, it is the major determinant of terminal wealth. The result of this kind of dispersion is the skewed distribution of wealth and the skewed distribution of the market values of corporations. It causes the skewed distribution of the assets, incomes, and dividends of corporations and of the wealth of individuals. It also partly causes the skewed distribution of the total assets of portfolios managed by trust departments, investment advisers, and mutual funds.

There is more. Not only is the distribution skewed, but it is skewed in a very regular way—one so regular that it can be described by a law. That law is known as Pareto's law of the distribution of income and wealth. In a more general form, the law is known as Zipf's law. Zipf, a Harvard psychologist, applied this law not to just economic factors but to the distribution of cities by size, to newspaper circulation, and to a host of other phenomena.

The law, applied to financial variables, is a variant of Pareto's distribution of income and wealth. It states: The cross-sectional distribution of any dollar financial variable becomes increasingly skewed with time and approaches the Pareto distribution.

How Does This Happen?

I first noticed the effect of this rule in looking at the distribution of assets in customers' stock portfolios when I was interested in reducing the risk in our customers' portfolios. As discussed in Chapter 8, you can reduce the risk in a stock portfolio by increasing the number of stocks, preferably using an equal investment in each stock. When I started looking at this matter, I assumed that the investments in each stock, while not equal, would have some rough degree of equality. On looking at a number of portfolios, I was surprised to discover that the distribution of assets among stocks was very unequal. The distortion was so great, in fact, that a single stock frequently accounted for 50 percent or more of the total value of the portfolio, even in portfolios that had 20 or more stocks. The degree of concentration in a single stock was so great that we measured concentration by counting the number of portfolios with more than half the assets in a single stock.

In searching for reasons for this high degree of concentration (and our customers' portfolios were probably typical) I came up with the obvious reasons: the capital gains tax, which discouraged sale of stocks with high gains and encouraged sale of stocks with losses; the presence of stocks coming from sale of family companies—stocks that often represented the bulk of the portfolio; reluctance on the part of the portfolio manager or the customer to sell stocks that had done well. These were valid causes of concentration, but they were not the only cause, or the major cause. The major reason was that some stocks rise in price and others fall—for a variety of reasons. This continual rising and falling of individual stock values causes the initial values of the stocks to spread out, or become dispersed. It is this dispersion that is described by the above law.

The best illustration of the law of the dispersion of wealth in the stock market is given by the Fisher and Lorie study of wealth ratios from the New York Stock Exchange. The data gives wealth ratios at various deciles. By assuming you have one stock at each decile from the 10th to the 90th, we obtain an approximation of how wealth returns become skewed. (The data are taken from the final period (last row) of Fisher and Lorie's

Table 3.) First, let's look at proportion of total assets represented by each decile in Table 16.1.

The largest stock consumes a larger and larger portion of the portfolio. At the start, each stock represented 11 percent of the portfolio. After one year, the largest holding represented 15 percent; after 10 years, 20 percent; and after 40 years, 38 percent. The smallest holding declines to 8 percent after a year, 4 percent after 10 years, and less than 1 percent after 40 years. You can see how the portfolio becomes skewed with time. A similar pattern is revealed by the cumulative holdings (Table 16.2).

The dominance of the top stocks increases with time. After 10 years, the top three stocks have increased their share from 33 percent to 50 percent. By the end of 40 years, the same three stocks constitute 77 percent of the total value of the portfolio.

Table 16.1   Estimated Distribution of Assets Represented by Various Stocks After Various Intervals of Time

	Percent of Total Holdings		
Number of Stocks	**After 1 Year**	**After 10 Years**	**After 40 Years**
1	15	20	38
2	13	16	23
3	11	14	16
4	11	12	10
5	10	11	7
6	10	9	4
7	9	8	2
8	9	6	1

Table 16.2   Estimated Distribution of Assets Represented by Various Stocks After Various Intervals of Time

	Cumulative Percent of Total Holdings		
Number of Stocks	**After 1 Year**	**After 10 Years**	**After 40 Years**
1	15	20	38
2	28	37	62
3	41	50	77
4	53	62	87
5	63	73	94
6	73	82	98
7	83	89	99
8	92	96	100
9	100	100	100

The actual data in Table 16.3 represent the actual dispersion of returns. We can estimate that dispersion using our market model and the formula for the standard deviation of a lognormal distribution. Let's assume that the standard deviation of changes in the logs of prices is 0.2 and we hold the stocks for 40 years. This gives the following distribution, shown in Table 16.3.

The simulated results in Table 16.3 have been estimated using the formula for the standard deviation of the wealth ratio for a lognormal distribution. We assumed the underlying distribution was lognormal. The percentiles were calculated using a normal distribution. The one-year standard deviation for the simulated data was 0.20, which is somewhat lower than the log of the one-year standard deviation/mean (1.55/1.15). Thus, we used the statistics for one year to estimate the wealth distribution after 40 years. Notice that the largest stock for the simulated distribution was 36 percent versus 38 percent for the actual. The second largest holding was 21 percent for the simulated versus 23 percent for the actual. The third largest was 14 percent versus 16 percent; fourth and fifth largest were the same, 10 percent versus 10 percent and 7 percent versus 7 percent. Clearly, for the bulk of the portfolio, the simulated distribution gives quite a good prediction of the actual.

The significance of these findings is that you can predict to an approximate degree what your portfolio will look like—in terms of the distribution of holdings—after 40 years if you place equal investments in 9 stocks. There are other implications. This means that we have described the market quite well. The same model should apply to the distribution of sales, earnings, or assets of corporations.

Table 16.3   Simulated Distribution of Assets Represented by Nine Stocks After 40 Years

| | ──────────── Percent of Total Holdings ──────────── | | | |
Number of Stocks	Simulated	Actual	Simulated Cumulative	Actual Cumulative
1	36	38	36	38
2	21	23	57	62
3	14	16	70	77
4	10	10	80	87
5	7	7	87	94
6	5	4	92	98
7	4	2	96	99
8	2	1	99	100
9	1	-	100	100

CHAPTER 17

Diversification Across Time

Scenario

At a meeting of a pension investment committee, the managing director of the bank trust department that invested the company pension money was explaining why it was important not to try to time the market.

"Between the end of World War II and 1991, an investment of $1.00 in common stocks grew to $22.42—provided you kept your money in the market the whole time. But if you had missed the 30 best months of that 46-year period, your $1.00 would be worth only $2.74. That is a difference in return of 2 percent versus 7 percent.

"Therefore," concluded the speaker, "it is extremely dangerous to attempt to time the market—and chance being out at the wrong time."

He went on to explain that stocks compounded at 12 percent over the last decade, but if you had missed the best five of 120 months, your return dropped to 8 percent—a substantial difference.

His point was well taken. I started to calculate the probability of missing those five months, but my calculator couldn't handle it. Instead, I decided to look at the data to see whether what I had heard made sense. In doing so, I discovered an interesting fact, one that is obvious once you think about it.

The distribution of returns over time is similar to the distribution of returns across stocks. In each case, it is a lognormal distribution. We can calculate the probability of any return. If we form a frequency distribution of returns, say of monthly changes in the logs of prices, we will get a distribution that is approximately normal. There will be many small changes—and a few large changes, both positive and negative.

What the bank officer had done was simply to look at the effect on the total return if the high returns were eliminated—if, that is, an investor were out of the market during the months of high returns. Missing the market at certain times has an enormous effect. I suspected that the effect would be similar to the cross-sectional dispersion of returns on individual stocks in a portfolio with the passage of time. Recall that, after half a century, the largest holding accounts for roughly half the total portfolio. I expected a similar effect when looking at the market. But I was wrong: it was of an entirely different magnitude, as I soon discovered.

One dollar invested in the Standard & Poor's 500 Index in 1891—a century ago—grew to $78.80 by 1991. That works out to an annual compound return of 4.5 percent. If you eliminated the 120 months of highest returns, the overall compound return became negative. You lost money. On the other hand, if you eliminated the 120 worst months, your annual compound return increased from 4.5 to 17 percent per annum, nearly a fourfold increase.

Clearly, the impact of the very high and extremely low returns—the tails of the distribution—is great. The impact is much greater on diversification over time than it is on diversification across securities whenever the lowest returns are eliminated. The reason this is true is that the returns across time are *multiplied* to get the overall return, and that has a profound effect when the low returns are taken out.

In a portfolio, the situation is different. The return on each stock affects that stock's value. The individual stocks are then *added* together to get the new value for the portfolio. The return is calculated from that new sum. Removing the low returns has much less effect.

The distinction between added and multiplied is very important. For the market, the effect is multiplicative. For the portfolio, the effect is additive. Even though the underlying mechanism is similar—a lognormal distribution—the effect is entirely different.

In mathematical terms, we can let the variable u represent the return, expressed as the first difference in the logs. We can let u_t represent the return in a particular month or year and u_s represent the return for a particular security. We then have the following:

$$\text{Portfolio Return} = \text{sum } (\exp u_s) \tag{17.1}$$

$$\text{Market Return} = \exp (\text{sum } u_t) \tag{17.2}$$

Equation (17.1) says sum (exp), while Equation (17.2) says exp (sum). If we have the two numbers 5 and 5, the first equation [sum (exp 5, exp 5)] gives us just under 300; the second [exp (5 + 5)] gives us 22,000. The effect of the two equations is very different.

Suppose the two variables, u_t and u_i, have the same mean and standard deviation and the same approximately normal distribution. Even though this is so, we have two very different situations. In Equation (17.1)—the portfolio—we have the sum of the exponents. In Equation (17.2)—the market over time—we have the exponent of the sum. For the latter (the market), the tails of the distribution have much greater impact on overall return because the effect is multiplicative, not additive. That point was dramatically made when you saw that, by eliminating the 120 worst months in the last century, the return increased *fourfold*.

It is not possible to prepare the same kind of table for diversification over time that we prepared for diversification across securities because the effect is multiplicative, not additive. Each component has a different effect, depending on the other components.

If you rank returns in descending order and look at the deciles, the effect becomes clear. We did that, converting these to returns to indicate what happens as you select the best months, years, and decades. The results are shown in Table 17.1.

The annual compound returns during the top decile months was 135 percent per year. For the bottom decile months, the return was -62 percent per year. In the best 10 years, the average return was 35 percent per year; in the worst 10 years it was -29. Choice by decades reduces the range from 12 percent for the top decade to -2 percent for the worst.

The drop in the dispersion of returns by deciles is due to the effect of averaging. The standard deviation of a mean is approximately equal to the mean divided by the square root of the number of items. It declines as you add more items. The annual return has 12 months, and the decade return has 120 months. Because you are taking the average of 12 months or 120 months instead of one month, the standard deviation declines and, with it, the degree of dispersion. This is evident in Table 17.1.

The impact is made even more dramatic if we show what an investment of $1.00 in each decile would become after a decade, using the deciles of monthly returns, ranked from highest to lowest. The result is given in Table 17.2. The top decile shows what results from the annual returns on $1.00 invested for a decade after picking the best 120 months, 10 years, or single decade. The bottom decile shows what results from picking the worst 120 months, 10 years, or single decade.

Given a return of 135 percent earned during the best months, an investment of $1.00 would be worth $5,132 at the end of 10 years. An investment in the 120 worst months would have reduced your $1.00 to less than a cent. Your total return over the 100 years would have been $78.80—the product of the amounts in the months column.

When we turn to the ranked by years column, we see that an investment of $1.00 in the best 10 years would have produced $21. The same investment in the worst 10 years would have reduced your dollar investment to 3 cents.

Table 17.2 differs greatly from the table showing diversification among various stocks. This is particularly evident in the months column.

Table 17.1   Annual Compound Return Ranked by Months, Years, and Decades, 1891–1991 Standard & Poor's 500

Decile Rank	Ranked by Months	Ranked by Years	Ranked by Decades
1	135	35	12
2	59	26	12
3	41	19	10
4	28	15	5
5	15	11	3
6	3	7	2
7	-7	0	1
8	-18	-8	1
9	-32	-15	0
10	-62	-29	-2

Table 17.2	Ending Wealth After 10 Years Investment Ranked by Months, Years, and Decade Deciles, 1891–1991 Standard & Poor's 500		
Decile Rank	**Ranked by Months**	**Ranked by Years**	**Ranked by Decades**
1	$5,132	$21	$3.1
2	106	10	3.1
3	32	6	2.7
4	12	4	1.6
5	4	3	1.4
6	1	2	1.3
7	0.5	1	1.2
8	.1	.4	1.1
9	.02	.2	1.0
10	.00	.03	.8

To time the market so as to achieve the most spectacular results would be very difficult, as suggested by the bank officer of our pension investment meeting, because there is a one in 10 chance of picking the best decade. But the probability of selecting the individual best 10 years out of 100 is less than one in 10 billion. The probability of choosing the best or worst 120 months out of 1,201 months would be far less.

If we had treated diversification over time, using the above data, like diversification over securities, the results would have been quite different. Doing so would reveal clearly the difference between the multiplicative effect of time and the additive effect of holding different stocks. We can make the simulation by assuming that we invest $1.00 each month (or each year, or decade) in the time period in question and then add the amounts together to produce the value of a portfolio. (The addition is in contrast with what actually happens when we multiply the results of each time period.)

We can compare the skewness produced by addition with what we obtained earlier. Using monthly returns, the best 120 months would have produced only 12 percent of the total portfolio. Using decade returns, the best decade of the 10 would have amounted to about 17 percent of the total portfolio—roughly the same figure we get with a portfolio of 10 stocks after 10 years and a 15 percent standard deviation. This is typical of the market standard deviation.

Clearly, proper timing could produce quite spectacular or quite dismal results. Attempting to pick the right time and being right or wrong has a far greater effect on return than stock selection. The more pronounced effect is due to the fact that returns over time are *multiplied* together to get the final gain or loss, not added up as in a portfolio.

CHAPTER 18

Predicting Dividend Changes

Dividend income is extremely important to several large classes of investors: individual investors seeking dividend yield, income-oriented trusts, and income-oriented common stock mutual funds. For these investors, the current dividend payment on common stock may not be an accurate measure of future yield because dividends continually are being increased and decreased. Despite the importance of forecasting future changes in dividend payments, there are remarkably few studies of it.

Dividend changes differ in important respects from changes in nearly all other financial variables. For many companies, dividends remain unchanged for long periods, such that the same dividend is paid year after year. For another and considerably larger group of companies, dividend changes are infrequent, less than one change every year or two. For a smaller group of companies, dividend changes are made quite regularly. Yet even in this last group, quarterly payments often remain unchanged for four quarters at a time. The net effect is that the odds of no dividend change are about four in 10, based on a sample of approximately 13,000 dividend changes over 19 years among industrial companies contained in the Compustat tapes.

Compared to changes in dividends, changes in other financial variables occur almost continuously. Earnings per share fluctuate constantly from quarter to quarter and from year to year. It is an unusual rather than common event when earnings go unchanged from one period to the next. Common stock prices shift continuously from day to day, week to week, and year to year.

Dividends differ from other financial variables in another respect. Dividend payments can be set by the company directors for most companies in most years. While company directors and company management cannot determine other financial variables, they can establish the current dividend payment, within the limitations imposed by earned income and by any debt covenants. It is this ability to set dividend payments that is largely responsible for the relative constancy of the dividend.

The major uncontrollable restraint is that dividends generally must be paid from current earnings. When earnings fall below the declared dividend, company directors will be forced to consider reducing the dividend. Otherwise, directors usually are reluctant to reduce the existing dividend rate.

The income-oriented investor generally is very concerned with security, in providing income, and in continuing that income. It would be very useful, therefore, to have an accurate model with which to predict dividend changes, particularly to forecast the probability of dividend increases and reductions.

The most commonly used model or rule of thumb is the coverage test. Coverage is computed by dividing earnings available for payment of dividends by the amount of the dividend paid. If earnings per share are $3.00 and the dividend payment is $1.50, coverage is computed by dividing $3.00 by $1.50, which gives a coverage ratio of 2.0 times. Thus, in this example, earnings available are 2.0 times the dividend payment.

Unfortunately, the coverage test has several weaknesses. It implicitly assumes a linear relationship between coverage and dividend safety, though the relationship is not linear. In fact, a dividend covered 2.2 times by earnings is 4.0 times less likely to be reduced the following year than a dividend covered 1.1 times by earnings.

In order to improve on the coverage ratio, Richard Johnson and I first examined dividend increases and reductions for 900 companies over the period 1948–1968. There were 1,750 dividend reductions over that period; of these, 1,400 were among stocks for which the coverage ratio was in excess of 1.0 (i.e., where the dividend payment *was covered* by earnings). The dividend was cut, even though earnings *exceeded* dividends. Furthermore, the payment was cut among a group of companies for which the overall incidence of reduction in dividends was not high.

Because the simple coverage test, as normally used, did not provide a systematic measure, we decided to use the reciprocal of the coverage ratio (i.e., the dividend payout ratio) to see whether that provided a more systematic relationship to dividend reductions

Table 18.1   Payout Ratio and Dividend Changes: 1949–1968

Payout Ratio	Increase %	Decrease %
10–19	80	6
20–29	79	7
30–39	73	8
40–49	65	10
50–59	48	12
60–69	38	14
70–79	22	20
80–89	17	27
90–99	14	40
100–109	14	44
110–119	6	61
Average	50	13

and also to examine dividend increases. If dividends are $1.50 and earnings are $3.00, the dividend payout ratio is 0.50, or 50 percent.

The results of our study are shown in Table 18.1, which gives the payout ratio and the percentages of increases and decreases in dividends.

As you can see, there is a systematic relationship between the payout ratio and the proportions of increases and decreases in the dividend.

For increases, there is an inverse relationship between the payout and the frequency of increases. The lower the payout, the higher the proportion of increases. This relationship may be stated in terms of the following formula, equating the proportion of decreases to the payout ratio.

$$\text{Percent of Increases} = 96 - (.84 \times \text{payout})$$

For the decreases, there is a direct relationship when you use the logs of the proportion of increases. In fact, if you plot the proportion of decreases on a log scale against payout on an arithmetic scale, you get a nearly straight line. The degree of explanation is very high (r-squared = 0.98). The log of proportion of decreases is a function of payout. The formula for this is:

$$\text{Percent of Decreases} = e^{1.2 + (.0245 \times \text{payout})}$$

In each of the above formulas, payout was expressed as a percent.

Table 18.1 excludes changes for payouts below 10 percent and above 120 percent where the sample was quite small and the proportion of cuts and increases was no longer a systematic function of payout. The frequency of dividend reduction does not rise when the payout is above 120 percent. When earnings are negative, the frequency of dividend reduction drops from over 50 percent to 33 percent.

The evidence in Table 18.1 makes it possible to estimate the probability of a dividend cut next year based on the payout last year. Also, you can estimate the probability of a dividend increase from the payout ratio.

Clearly, dividend reduction is a direct function of payout for payout ratios extending from 10 percent to 120 percent, and dividend increase is an inverse function of payout. The direct relationship between payout and dividend reduction makes it possible to forecast the probability of dividend reductions. Similar forecasts can be made about dividend increases.

CHAPTER 19

The Basis for Predicting the Probability of Loss

The question of profit or loss is extremely important, both to large and small companies. For instance, losses ultimately drove Penn Central to file for bankruptcy in 1972. Banks and investors alike lost hundreds of millions of dollars in defaulted loans and plummeting market values. But losses do not always lead to bankruptcy. More often than not, losses are temporary, particularly among large corporations.

Even these temporary losses have adverse effects. However, in the years and months preceding a deficit, market declines can be substantial. Credit ratings are adjusted downward, thus hurting bond prices, sometimes severely. The equity shrinks and, with it, the ability to meet coupon or principal payments. The firm's financial structure weakens, and the dividend may be placed in jeopardy. Profitable firms do not normally suffer these disadvantages. They can usually make remittances to creditors, meet dividend and coupon payments, repay principal, and retain satisfactory credit ratings.

Despite the importance of the question of future profit or loss, to my knowledge, few systematic studies on the prediction of firm profit or loss have been published.

Profits of the firm represent the result of an extremely complex process involving the exchange of goods and services for money. The participants include members of the firm, suppliers, customers, investors, and lenders. Each exchange usually represents a fair trade between buyer and seller. The very nature of this process leads you to expect a profit series of differences characterized by a normal distribution, a zero mean, and a rate of diffusion or standard deviation that increases with the square root of the differencing or time interval. This is the same process described by the fourth law. The evidence also reveals that successive percentage changes in earnings are uncorrelated, as stated by the second law (see Chpater 27).

We defined profits as the ratio of net income to total assets. This measure proved superior to any of 45 other measures of profit in distinguishing future profit firms from future loss firms. Using this measure, we created a series of changes in profits that were found by subtracting profits in one year from profits in the following year. We then divided profits in the latest year by the standard deviation of the changes in profits in the prior year. This gave us a dimensionless variable, the z-score. Having calculated the z-statistic, we can calculate the probability of profit or loss from tables of the normal distribution.

To test the accuracy of the estimates for individual firms, we calculated probabilities of profit and loss for a large number of firms in a given year, based on data available in the prior year. Then we classified the firms by estimated probability of loss and compared estimated frequencies with actual frequencies. The data were taken from the Compustat tapes for the years 1965–1976; the total sample was 1,343 firms. The results are shown in Table 19.1.

Table 19.1 shows the marked correlation between the z-score in one year and the proportion of firms realizing losses in the following year. The lower the z-score, the higher the proportion of losses, rising from about 1 percent of all firms with high z-scores to 24 percent of all firms with low z-scores and 43 percent for negative z-scores (firms already unprofitable). Thus, the method effectively groups firms on the basis of future frequency of loss.

Clearly, this model is useful for estimating the probability that a company will make or lose money in the future. Because the method homogenizes the data, making it dimensionless, ratings of companies in one industry are directly comparable with ratings of companies in other industries and ratings of small companies are comparable with ratings of large companies. For example, the ratings can be used to compare a bank with a utility company, a retail firm with a chemical firm, an airline with a farm implement company, or a small, local firm with General Motors.

Table 19.1	Frequency of Loss among Firms Previously Classified by Probability of Loss					
Class in One Year **Z-Score**	**A**	**B**	**C**	**D**	**E**	**F**
From	2.4	1.4	1.15	0.55	0.0	- inf
To	inf	2.4	1.4	1.15	0.55	0.0
Loss in next year	48	47	22	48	72	165
Profit in next year	4,585	639	242	329	297	222
Percent loss	1.1	7.4	9.1	14.7	24.2	43.0

CHAPTER 20

The Importance of Dividends

The common view is that the major portion of stock market returns come from capital appreciation. That view is generally correct in the short run. For example, when the standard deviation of stock market returns is 18 percent, the 3 percent to 5 percent yield as often as not contributes only a small part of the return over a one- or two-year period. Capital appreciation, or capital depreciation, has the major influence.

But when we look at longer periods, the effect of dividends becomes much more significant. The importance of dividends is illustrated vividly by the data in Table 20.1, which show dividend returns and capital appreciation returns from common stocks from 1790–1985.

On the basis of these data, dividends were a more important source of return than capital appreciation in the majority of decades. The dividend returns shown for the last decade of the eighteenth century and for most of the nineteenth century were simulated and are therefore less accurate. Taking only the twentieth century data, we see that dividends provided greater returns than capital appreciation in four decades whereas capital appreciation was dominant in six. Thus, dividends were extremely important in well over half of the decades in both centuries and in slightly less than half of the twentieth century.

Over the total period 1790–1985, capital appreciation provided a 3.2 percent compound annual return. Dividend income provided a 5.0 percent return. Here, the dividends outranked capital appreciation in importance.

Another way to look at the importance of dividends is to examine the index value of $1.00 invested in 1789 and held to the twentieth century under two conditions: when there were no dividends and when there were.

The importance of dividends can be seen in Table 20.2, which shows the indexes at the ends of various decades under income return alone, capital appreciation, and total return.

The original investment of $1.00 was made in 1759. By 1985, the capital appreciation would have increased the investment to $441, the income return would have been $11,230, and the total return would have been $4,953,173. Thus, without income, the

Table 20.1   Comparison of Dividend and Capital Appreciation Returns: 1790–1985 (percent per year)

Period	Capital Appreciation	Dividend Return	Greater Source
1790–1799	5.3	5.1	Apprec.
1800–1809	3.7	5.3	Div.
1810–1819	4.0	5.1	Div.
1820–1829	1.8	5.0	Div.
1830–1839	-2.6	5.1	Div.
1840–1849	4.0	5.1	Div.
1850–1859	-4.0	5.1	Div.
1860–1869	10.9	5.0	Apprec.
1870–1879	2.1	6.0	Div.
1880–1889	0.8	4.9	Div.
1890–1899	1.3	4.2	Div.
1900–1909	5.5	4.2	Apprec.
1910–1919	-1.4	5.5	Div.
1920–1929	7.3	5.6	Apprec.
1930–1939	-5.0	5.2	Div.
1940–1949	3.5	6.0	Div.
1950–1959	12.7	5.5	Apprec.
1960–1969	4.5	3.7	Apprec.
1970–1979	1.9	4.3	Div.
1980–1985	12.0	4.7	Apprec.

Adapted with permission from Ibbotson, R. and Brinson, G., *Investment Markets: Gaining the Performance Advantage*, McGraw Hill, New York, 1986, Table 5.6, page 77.

return was considerably lower. The average annual capital appreciation return was 3.2 percent, the average annual income return was 5.0 percent, and the total return was 8.2 percent. In the twentieth century, when capital appreciation was relatively greater, income returns were less important but nonetheless very important to total returns.

Clearly, for the market as a whole, dividends provide an important source of return. In some decades, dividends represented the more important source of return. In other decades, capital appreciation was the more important source. The total realized return was far less without dividends than with dividends. Consequently, dividends play an extremely important role in the total return achievable by investment in common stocks.

| Table 20.2 | Comparison of Capital Appreciation and Total Return: 1789–1985 |

Year	Income Return Index	Capital Appreciation Index	Total Return Index
1790	1.0	1.0	1.0
1800	1.7	1.7	2.7
1810	2.6	2.4	6.4
1820	4.2	3.6	15.2
1830	6.0	4.3	29.4
1840	11.3	3.3	37.5
1850	18.3	4.9	89.9
1860	30.7	3.3	100.3
1870	47.9	9.2	440.0
1880	84.9	11.3	955.8
1890	136.5	12.2	1,661.7
1900	205.0	13.8	2,829.0
1910	518.4	23.6	7,153.3
1920	522.7	20.4	10,674.0
1930	873.7	41.2	35,996.0
1940	1,424.0	24.7	35,130.8
1950	2,506.6	34.9	87,354.7
1960	4,042.1	115.1	465,087.6
1970	5,539.0	184.4	1,021,227.8
1980	8,762.7	223.5	1,958,108.6
1985	11,230.4	441.1	4,953,173.4

Adapted with permission from Ibbotson, R. and Brinson, G., *Investment Markets: Gaining the Performance Advantage*, McGraw Hill, New York, 1986, Table 5.6, page 77.

CHAPTER 21

Estimating the Standard Deviation from High and Low Stock Prices

In this chapter, we examine an alternate method of estimating the major measure of the volatility of a stock's price, the *standard deviation*. Normally, the standard deviation is estimated from closing prices—daily, weekly, monthly, or annually. An alternate method, one rarely used, is to estimate the standard deviation from high and low prices, which may also be daily, weekly, monthly, or annually. This method has two advantages:

1. High and low prices often are available in publications when closing prices are not.

2. The high/low price contains more information than the closing price and therefore gives a more reliable estimate of the standard deviation.

In discussing the high/low method, we first describe the normal method of computing the standard deviation from closing prices so that the difference between the two methods can be seen clearly.

The Normal Method of Calculating the Standard Deviation from the Change in the Closing Price

In the preceding chapters, we have shown how to estimate the standard deviation of a stock's price from changes in the natural logarithms of price. Using monthly data, for example, we subtract the price at the end of one month from the price at the end of the following month. This procedure gives us a series of monthly changes in the price of the stock. Instead of using the actual prices of the stock, we use the natural logarithms of the prices. The normal method of computing the standard deviation from monthly data using month-end prices is as follows:

1. Compute the monthly returns in natural logarithms by subtracting the natural log of the ending price from the natural log of the beginning price.

2. Repeat this for each monthly interval. The difference in logs is the logarithmic monthly return. The formula for this calculation is:

    Monthly Return = Nat. Log. Ending Price – Nat. Log. Beginning Price

    This formula gives us a series of price changes measured in logs, or log differences, as shown in column 3 of Table 21.1. The log difference is actually the monthly return.

3. Compute the mean of the log differences shown in column 3. The total log difference is the sum of column 3, or 0.96. The mean log difference is 0.96 divided by the number of items in column 3, or 9, which gives a mean change of 0.106 or 0.10.

4. To obtain the values in column 4, subtract the mean of 0.10 from the corresponding item in column 3.

5. Square each item in column 4, and place the result in column 5.

6. Finally, compute the total of the squared items of column 5, which is 0.1014. That is the variance of the changes in the logs of prices. The square root of that number is the standard deviation, which is 0.113. The exponent of 0.113 is 1.119, which, expressed in percent, is 11.9 percent. Thus, the standard deviation computed from the monthly changes in the logs of the closing prices is 11.9 percent.

The above figures may not come out precisely due to rounding of data shown in Table 21.1.

Calculating the Standard Deviation from High and Low Prices

When using the high/low method of estimating the standard deviation of changes in prices, we use the range between the high and low prices in each period instead of the actual change in price during the period. This method, first described by Michael Parkinson and based on work by William Feller, provides a superior estimate, since the high/low range contains more information than the closing price.

The rationale for using high and low prices to calculate the standard deviation is based on the notion that the price of an individual stock follows a random walk, at least to a very good approximation. The variance of the rate of return is what Parkinson called the

Table 21.1	Calculating the Standard Deviation from the Change in the Closing Price: S&P 500, 1983–1992

	Price (1)	Log Price (2)	Log Dif. (3)	Log Dif. (4)	Col. 4 Squared (5)
1992	436	6.07	.04	-.06	.004
1991	417	6.03	.23	.13	.016
1990	330	5.80	-.07	-.17	.031
1989	353	5.87	.24	-.13	.017
1988	278	5.63	.12	.01	.000
1987	247	5.51	.02	-.09	.008
1986	242	5.49	.14	.03	.001
1985	211	5.35	.23	.13	.016
1984	167	5.12	.01	-.10	.009
1983	165	5.11			

Sum of Column 3	0.96	
Mean of Column 3	0.106	
Sum of Column 5		0.1014
Mean of Sum of Column 5 $.1014/(n - 1) = .1014/8$ =		0.0127
Square Root of .0127 =		Standard Deviation
=		0.113
or, in Percent =		11.9%

diffusion constant. The standard deviation is simply the square root of the variance (or diffusion constant).

Instead of calculating the standard deviation by examining the changes in the natural logarithms of prices, we can measure differences between the natural logarithms of high and low prices. These differences should give a good estimate of the standard deviation, since the average difference will get larger or smaller as the standard deviation gets larger or smaller.

Table 21.2   Calculation of Standard Deviation from Annual High and Low Prices: S&P 500, 1983–1992

	High Price (1)	Low Price (2)	Log High Price (3)	Log Low Price (4)	Natural Log Range (5)	Square of Natural Log Range (6)
1992	441	395	6.09	5.98	.11	.012
1991	417	312	6.03	5.74	.29	.084
1990	369	296	5.91	5.69	.22	.049
1989	360	275	5.89	5.62	.27	.073
1988	284	243	5.65	5.49	.16	.024
1987	337	224	5.82	5.41	.41	.167
1986	254	204	5.54	5.32	.22	.048
1985	212	164	5.36	5.10	.26	.066
1984	170	148	5.14	5.00	.14	.019
1983	173	138	5.15	4.93	.23	.051

Sum of Squares of Natural Log Ranges   .593

Variance   =   .361 x (1/n) x Sum of Squares
                                       =   .361 x (1/10) x .593
                                       =   .0214

where n is the number of observations (in this case, 10).

Standard Deviation   =   Square Root of Variance
                                       = $.0214^2$
                                       =   0.146
or, in Percent   =   15.7%

The derivation of the probability distribution of high/low values for a continuous random walk has been published by Feller and results in the formula:

$$\text{Variance} = (0.361/n) \times \text{Square Root of Sum } [\ln(\text{high}/\text{low})]^2$$

where n is the number of observations and ln is the symbol for natural logarithm.

The high/low method is much more sensitive than the closing-price method to variations in the standard deviation. In using the high/low method, we calculate the difference between the high price and the low price of the stock during the month. We then use this range instead of the actual change in price during the month. The calculation is as follows:

Month's Range = High Price – Low Price

In practice, we calculate the difference in the natural logs between the high and low prices.

Range = Nat. Log. High Price – Nat. Log. Low Price

Variance = .361 × (1/n) × (Sum [Range squared])

Standard Deviation = Square Root of Variance

The procedure is shown in Table 21.2.

To express the standard deviation in percent, we take the exponent of 0.146, or 1.157, which is a standard deviation of 15.7 percent.

To show the comparative results of using the two methods, the normal closing-price method and the high/low method, we have calculated the standard deviation using each method for the Standard & Poor's 500 Index for seven 10-year periods between 1923–1992. The results are shown in Table 21.3.

Note that these data clearly reveal a close correlation between the standard deviations produced by the two methods.

We also have calculated the standard deviation of the Standard & Poor's 500 using annual high, low, and closing prices for the entire period 1918–1992. The results are shown in the last line of Table 21.3. As can be seen, changes in the natural logarithms of the closing prices gave a standard deviation of 0.190 while the high/low method gave a standard deviation of 0.196, a difference of only 0.006.

Table 21.3   Comparison of High/Low Price and Closing-Price Calculations of the Standard Deviation: 1923–1992, S&P 500 Standard Deviation in Natural Logarithms

| | **Method Used in Calculation** | | |
Period	High/Low Price	Closing Price	Difference
1923–32	.30	.32	-.02
1933–42	.27	.23	.04
1943–52	.13	.12	.01
1953–62	.15	.19	-.04
1963–72	.12	.11	.01
1973–82	.17	.20	-.03
1983–92	.15	.11	.04
1918–92	.190	.196	-.006

According to Parkinson, for a given level of error, five times as much data are required to calculate the variance from the closing price as from high and low prices. Thus, to get a given accuracy using the high/low method, we need about 80 percent less data (and thus, an 80 percent smaller time interval). In practice, the difference is probably less. In any case, the estimate of the standard deviation derived from the high/low method may be expected to have a much smaller error than that calculated from the closing-price method.

CHAPTER 22

Rescaled Range (R/S) Analysis

The *rescaled range* refers to a statistical ratio that has been recently applied to stock and bond prices in an attempt to detect the presence of trends. The ratio is computed by dividing the range (R) of stock prices, for example, by the standard deviation of changes in stock prices (S), hence the definition. In practice, the logs of prices are used to calculate the range and the mean change is deducted, as described later in this chapter. The analysis consists of examining how the R/S statistic changes with changes in the time interval over which the range is measured. The relationship of these two variables is said to enable one to detect the presence, or absence, of trends.

R/S analysis has been used both to assert that stock prices are random and to assert quite the opposite—that they are not random but exhibit some evidence of trend. Included in the latter view is the argument that stock prices are a form of *fractal* phenomena, or a series that exhibits evidence of self-similarity but is not strictly random.

Rescaled range analysis was first developed by H. E. Hurst in studies of the Nile River. Hurst was interested in knowing how high or low the water level might be, knowledge critical to dam construction and the regulation of water levels in Egypt. He measured the difference between the highest and lowest levels of water over a set of years, such as a decade. That calculation gave him the range of levels in that time period. Then, to homogenize the data, Hurst measured the range, not in terms of the number of feet but in terms of the natural logarithms of feet. After subtracting the mean change, he divided the range, R, by the standard deviation, S, of annual changes in the natural logarithms of the levels. That calculation gave him an R/S value for that period. Next, Hurst calculated the same measure for other decades, using precisely the same procedure. He then averaged the R/S figures for all of the separate years, giving him a mean R/S for a 10-year period.

He performed the same procedure for different numbers of years, 11, 12, . . . ,*n*. Once he had the R/S for different length periods, Hurst turned to his major question: What was the relationship between the R/S value and the number of years, *n*? He knew that if changes in the level of water—the ranges—were random, the log of R/S should rise with the square root of the log of the number of months. In fact, the rate was not 0.5 but more like 0.7, indicating some persistence or trend in the data.

The very same R/S analysis has been applied to other phenomena, including the stock market. For the stock market, we take the range of a stock's price, the difference in the logs between the high and low monthly closing prices, minus the average price, and divide by the standard deviation of the logs of the monthly changes in price. This gives us the R/S ratio (Range/Standard Deviation) for a 12-month period. We repeat this for 12-month periods in other years and then calculate the average of the several R/Ss that we have computed. Next, we perform the same procedure for other lengths of periods (24 months, 36 months, etc.).

Once this has been done, we can examine the relationship between the log of R/S and the log of n. We expect the log of R/S to rise as the log of n is raised to the 0.5 power. For a random series, the exponent should be 0.5. If the exponent is greater than 0.5, there is some persistence in the data, or a long-run trend of some sort. If the exponent is less than 0.5, there is a tendency for increases to be followed by decreases and vice versa.

Thus, by examining the relationship between the ratio R/S and the number of periods (i.e., time intervals), n, over which the range R is measured, we can tell whether the series has a persistent trend (upward or downward), is periodic, or is random. For a series with a trend, the log of R/S rises at a rate greater than $n^{0.5}$ but no greater than $n^{1.0}$. For a periodic series—one in which increases are followed by decreases and vice versa—R/S rises at a rate less than 0.5 after completion of the first cycle.

On reflection, we can see why this is so. In computing R/S, we calculate the standard deviation s from log differences in the smallest length period, $n = 1$. But we calculate the range, R, over n periods. For a homogeneous series, the standard deviation is more or less like a constant. Consequently, the rise in R/S comes almost entirely from increases in the range. Therefore, we can understand how R/S behaves as we increase n by looking only at the range.

Edgar Peters tested various series using the procedure described below. For the Standard & Poor's 500 daily from one day to 80 days, he found Hurst exponents that ranged from 0.57 to 0.62 over the period 1928–1989, indicating some persistence. Using different sampling procedures, Ambrose, Ancel, and Griffiths found Hurst exponents of 0.55 and 0.53 for the daily Standard & Poor's 500 from mid-1962 to the close of 1988. Peters concluded that there was some evidence of persistence in periods of less than four years; the other authors who used much longer periods concluded that there was no significant persistence and that the series was essentially random. The difference in results may lie partly in the different sampling techniques used and in the amount of data employed in each test.

The R/S procedure gives results that may be expected to be similar to the more straightforward analysis of the standard deviation and how it increases as the differencing interval is increased, as, for example, in going from monthly to annual changes. In Chapter 22, we have shown that the standard deviation may be computed from the range, R. In Chapter 5, we showed that the standard deviation, s, rises with the square root of time, or with an exponent of 0.5. Recall that it is the extreme values, the high and low prices, that the range embodies and that have a major influence on the calculation of the standard deviation. The major influence arises from the effect of squaring in calculating the stand-

Table 22.1   Hurst Coefficient for Log of R/S versus Log of *n*

Series	Non-Overlapping Data	Overlapping Data
Stocks		
General Motors, 1992 Daily	0.53	0.59
General Motors, 1991 Daily	0.50	0.47
Exxon, 1992 Daily	0.50	0.46
Dow Jones Average, 1992 Daily	0.57	0.71
Dow Jones Average, 1991 Daily	0.62	0.72
S&P 500, 1871–1991 Monthly Avg.	0.60	0.63
S&P 500, 1918–1992 Annual	0.71	0.59
NYSE, 1790–1992 Annual	0.51	0.60
Bond Yield Indexes, 1950–1992 Monthly		
U.S. Govt Yields 1-Year Monthly	0.66	0.67
U.S. Govt Yields 20-Year Monthly	0.62	0.57
Random Series		
Random Series #1	0.60	0.73
Random Series #2	0.60	0.73

ard deviation. As a result, much of the variation in s arises from the variation in the range, R.

We looked at several different series of stock prices to examine the coefficients. In doing so, we calculated R/S in periods ranging from $n = 7$ to $n = 50$ and computed the relationship between log R/S and log n. Table 22.1 gives the results. We have used both overlapping and non-overlapping data in computing the Hurst coefficient. The overlapping procedure uses every possible unique combination of the data.

As can be seen in Table 22.1, there is wide variation in the coefficient. General Motors showed little persistence in 1991 but, based on overlapping data, gave evidence of some in 1992. Exxon revealed none in 1992. The Dow Jones Industrials—again based on daily data—revealed persistence in 1991 and 1992, particularly on the basis of overlapping data. The Standard & Poor's 500 monthly data revealed persistence over the 1871–1991 period as did the annual New York Stock Exchange series (NYSE)—based on overlapping data only—over the two-century span from 1790 to 1992. For U.S. government yields, there was evidence of a trend for both the one-year bonds and the 20-year bonds. For the random series, we obtain coefficients of 0.60 with non-overlapping data and .73 with overlapping data. In the non-overlapping method of computation, the Hurst coefficients began at high levels and declined as the number of intervals of increasing length rose. In the overlapping method, the coefficients declined to .46 and then rose again .73.

Method of Calculating the R/S Ratio

The following example (see Table 22.2) describes the method of calculating the R/S ratio:

1. Suppose we have a long series of annual data. Select an interval of time, say 10 years of closing prices (column 1).

2. Take the logs of the prices (column 2).

3. Take the first difference in logs of the prices (column 3).

4. Compute the standard deviation, S, of the first differences.

5. Subtract from the first differences in the logs their mean (column 4).

6. Create a running sum of the first 10 months of log differences (column 5).

7. Subtract the minimum of that running sum from the maximum to obtain the range, R.

8. Divide R by S to obtain R/S for the first 10 months.

9. Repeat this process for all other 10-month sets of intervals.

10. Take the mean of the R/S values, which gives the R/S for 10 months ($n = 10$).

11. Repeat this process for other intervals ($n = 11, 12, ...$).

12. Plot the log of R/S against the log of n. The slope of the line and the regression coefficient give the Hurst (R/S) exponent, which states the rate of increase in the log of R/S with increases in the log of n. For a random series, the slope should be 0.5.

Calculations may be slightly different due to rounding.

Conclusion

The Hurst exponent—or the rate at which the log of the R/S ratio rises with the log of the number of periods, n, under different methods of measurement for stock prices, bond yields, and certain other financial series—is characterized by the following features:

Table 22.2   Calculation of R/S: S&P 500 Closing Prices, 1980–1990

	Price	Log of Price	Log Difference	Cumulative of (3)	Running Sum of Column 4
	(1)	**(2)**	**(3)**	**(4)**	**(5)**
1990	330	5.80	-.07	-.159	-.159
1989	353	5.87	.24	.151	-.008
1988	278	5.63	.12	.031	.023
1987	247	5.51	.02	-.069	-.046
1986	242	5.49	.14	.051	.005
1985	211	5.35	.23	.141	.146
1984	167	5.12	.01	-.079	.067
1983	165	5.11	.16	.071	.138
1982	141	4.95	.14	.051	.189
1981	123	4.81	-.10	-.189	.000
1980	136	4.91			

Range of Logs of Prices in Column 5 $= .159 - (-.189)$ $= .348$

Standard Deviation of Log Difference (Column 3) $= 0.1176$

R/S = Range/Standard Deviation $= .348/.1176$ $= 2.96$

1.   As the number of periods, n, increases, the Hurst exponent declines.

2.   As the beginning value of n decreases, the Hurst exponent increases; conversely, as the beginning value of n increases, the Hurst exponent declines toward 0.5.

3.   There is considerable variation in the Hurst exponent in different historical periods and different series.

Overall, the data suggest that there is sometimes evidence of trends, sometimes evidence of periodicity, and sometimes evidence of pure randomness, all depending on the time of measurement, the method used, and the particular series measured. In addition, since there is considerable variation in the range, with the extreme outliers of any distribution being the most erratic in behavior, we may expect to have inconsistent results.

CHAPTER 23

Options: Estimating Probable Price Changes in Evaluating Options

In buying or selling options, the probability of profit or loss depends on the probability of changes in price of the underlying stock. If we pay $1 to obtain the right to buy a stock at $105 within the next month, and the current price of the stock is $100, we will make a profit if the stock rises above $106. That's a 6 percent increase in price. The probability of the stock rising 6 percent depends on the time interval within which we have the opportunity to exercise the option and the standard deviation of changes in that particular stock's price. If the stock has an annual standard deviation of 25 percent and we have 30 days to exercise, the probability of a price rise of 6 percent during that 30 days is 18 percent. If we have 90 days to exercise the same stock at the same price, the probability of a 6 percent rise in price is 30 percent.

The probability of earning a return depends on the standard deviation of the stock, the time interval within which the option must be exercised, and the probability distribution of stock price changes. For most stocks, the normal distribution may be used to approximate the distribution of the logs of price changes.

In this chapter, we show how to estimate the probability of stock price changes that may be used in evaluating the purchase of options. We begin first with a brief description of some of the features of options. Then we turn to a description of how to use Table 23.1 and Appendix III to estimate the probability of price changes of various magnitudes for stocks with different standard deviations. The procedure is the same as used in earlier chapters, except that, for options, the time periods involved are generally no more than 90 days.

A Description of Options

In return for a small fee, a *stock option* grants the buyer the right to purchase, or sell, the stock at a fixed price within a specified length of time. A *call option* grants the purchaser the right to *call* (i.e., buy) the stock at a given price within a given period of time. A *put option*, on the other hand, grants the purchaser the right to *put* (i.e., sell) the stock, again, at a given price within a given period of time. The price at which the stock is to be purchased or sold in the future is called the *exercise price* or *strike price*.

The date on which the option expires, after which it cannot be exercised, is called the *expiration date*. Generally puts and calls have expiration dates that are three, six, or nine months from initiation. European puts and calls differ from American puts and calls in that the European variety can be exercised only on the expiration date, not anytime before.

In the United States, exercise prices are at standardized intervals of $2.50, $5, and $10. Options expire at standardized dates of 30, 60, and 90 days. Options are for 100 shares of stock.

For example, if IBM were selling at $96⅞, a call expiring in February to buy stock at $95 might be priced at $2⅞. The call would give the buyer of the call the right to purchase IBM at $95 through the end of February.

Note that the call price of $2⅞ exceeds the difference between the current price of IBM ($96⅞) and the exercise price ($95). If the buyer of the call exercised the option immediately, his or her loss would equal the selling price of $96⅞ less the cost of the shares, $95, and the cost of the call, $2⅞. The net proceeds on the transaction would be $96⅞ – ($95 + 2 ⅞) = -$1.00. The buyer of the call should expect to profit from a rise in the price of IBM prior to the end of February when the call expires.

A call expiring at the end of March might be priced at $4⅜ and one at the end of April, $5½.

Two features of these examples illustrate two rules of options:

1. The call price always exceeds the difference between the stock price and the exercise price.

2. Options with more distant expiration dates always have higher prices than options with earlier expiration dates.

    If the call price plus the exercise price were less than the current price, the buyer of the option could reap an immediate profit by buying the option, exercising it to obtain the stock, and then selling the stock. If, in the above example, the February option were priced at $1 instead of $2⅞, the option buyer could buy the call option for $1, pay $95 for the stock (a total of $96), and then sell the stock for $96⅞, giving a profit of $⅞ per share. In practice, you should always sell the option rather than exercise it, buy the stock, and then sell the stock. This guideline holds for puts as well as calls.

    Rule 2 above arises from two considerations. First, if a near-term option is priced higher than a more distant option, it is possible to arbitrage and make a profit.

Second, the probability of a given rise in the stock price is higher for longer intervals, as we have seen. The standard deviation rises with the square root of time. Therefore, the further out the expiration date, the greater the opportunity for profit.

The above examples concern the prices of call options for different expiration dates but the same exercise price. For the same stock, IBM, priced at $96⅞, February call prices of $90, $95, $100, and $105 might be (respectively) $6⅝, $2⅞, $⅞, and $¼. Note two things: first, the differences in call prices are less than the differences in exercise prices. All of the above exercise prices differ by $5, more than any of the call prices. Second, the option price is inversely related to the call price. In other words:

3. The difference in call prices is always less than the difference in exercise prices.

4. Call prices are higher for lower exercise prices. (But the reverse is true for put prices; the lower the exercise price, the lower the put price.)

In deciding when or whether to buy an option, it is important to know the probability that the stock price will rise or fall by a certain amount. We can determine the probabilities of given percentage rises or falls in the same way we determined probabilities of changes in profit margins and other variables. The first thing we need to know about a call is the price increase needed to give you a profit.

Estimating the Probability of
Stock Price Changes for a Call

To determine the percentage rise in price on a call option needed to achieve a profit, we must add to the exercise price, or strike price, the cost of buying the option and then divide that sum by the current price of the stock. If the current price of the stock is $100, the exercise price is $105, and the cost of the option is $1, the stock has to exceed $106 before we can earn a profit. That works out to a 6 percent rise in the price of the stock.

Suppose the stock has an annual standard deviation of 30 percent, and the option expires in five days. (All standard deviations in the tables are expressed on an annual basis.) In Table 23.1, we can see that the probability of a 6 percent rise in the price of a stock is 3 percent. We obtain this number in Table 23.1 by looking down the column under a standard deviation of 30 percent and across the 6 percent row to see a figure of 3 percent for the probability. Thus, the probability of a 6 percent or greater rise in five days is only 3 percent.

If we have 30 days to expiration, we use Table IIIe of Appendix III. In that table, we see that the probability of a 6 percent rise in price is 22 percent. This analysis assumes an equal probability of a rise or fall in the price of the stock. It may be that we think the stock's expected mean rise is 5 percent. In that case, we can adjust the figure and still use the table. To do so, subtract the expected mean rise of 5 percent from the 6 percent required for a profit, which leaves a rise of 1 percent. The probability of a 1 percent rise in five days is 37 percent.

Table 23.1   **Probabilities of Gain or Loss 5 Days in the Future**
for Various Standard Deviations

Annual Standard Deviation (%)

Increase/ Decrease (%)	5	10	15	20	25	30	35	40	45	50
			Probability of Increase Greater than Shown							
15	0	0	0	0	0	0	0	0	0	0
10	0	0	0	0	0	0	0	1	1	2
9	0	0	0	0	0	0	1	1	2	3
8	0	0	0	0	0	1	1	3	4	5
7	0	0	0	0	0	1	3	4	6	8
6	0	0	0	0	1	3	5	7	9	11
5	0	0	0	1	3	6	8	11	13	15
4	0	0	1	3	7	10	13	16	18	20
3	0	0	4	8	13	17	20	23	25	27
2	0	4	11	18	22	26	29	31	32	34
1	4	19	27	32	35	37	39	40	41	42
0	50	50	50	50	50	50	50	50	50	50
			Probability of Decrease Greater than Shown							
0	50	50	50	50	50	50	50	50	50	50
-1	4	18	27	32	35	37	39	40	41	42
-2	0	4	11	17	22	26	28	30	32	34
-3	0	0	3	8	12	16	19	22	24	26
-4	0	0	1	3	6	9	12	15	17	19
-5	0	0	0	1	2	5	7	10	12	14
-6	0	0	0	0	1	2	4	6	8	10
-7	0	0	0	0	0	1	2	3	5	6
-8	0	0	0	0	0	0	1	2	3	4
-9	0	0	0	0	0	0	0	1	2	2

Table 23.1 and Appendix III are built around a mean change in stock prices of zero, but other mean expected changes can be taken into account. For most stocks in most periods, the mean expected rise is 0 percent.

Estimating the Probability of
Stock Price Changes for a Put

In evaluating whether to purchase a put, consider the probability of a fall in price. The put enables us to sell the stock within a specified period at a certain price. If the price of the stock falls by more than that amount, we can buy the stock at below the put exercise price, sell it at the exercise price, and make a profit. The profit will be the difference between the exercise price and the future price, less the cost of the put. In practice, we would simply sell the put since its value will reflect our profit.

If the current price of the stock is $100, the exercise price is $90, and the cost of the put is $1, then the stock must drop by $11 or more ($100 – $90 – $1) in order to achieve a profit. That is an 11 percent drop in price. If the stock standard deviation is 30 percent and there are 30 days to expiration, the probability of an 11 percent drop is 6 percent, as shown in Table IIIe of Appendix III.

In conclusion, we can use Appendix III to determine the probability of a rise or fall in price of various percentages over selected periods. We can use that information to evaluate the probability that we will make a profit from the purchase of a put or call option. The tables in Appendix III do not provide our expected profit, but only the probability that the price will change enough in the right direction to give us a profit. The actual probability of profit depends on the expected value of the profit to be realized. If we have a 25 percent chance of winning a lottery and the payoff is over four times the cost, our expected gain is positive. Appendix III only tells us the probability of winning, not the expected gain.

CHAPTER 24

Betas Don't Work Very Well for Individual Stocks

In the 1960s, several researchers postulated a relationship between changes in the market and changes in the price of a stock. Specifically, these researchers believed that rates of change in the price of a stock were a function of rates of change in a market index. This belief reflected the fact that, when the market rises, the prices of most stocks rise and vice versa. The fact that the prices of individual stocks rise and fall with the market reflects that all stocks tend to move together in the same direction. Given a sharp upward turn of the market, most stocks move up; the reverse takes place when the market declines. These trends are obvious both to careful observers of the market and to professionals.

Researchers of the 1960s then postulated that the price changes of each stock were systematically related to the price changes of the market. Specifically, some stocks always moved more than the market moved, up or down. If the market rose 10 percent, stock **x** rose at 1.2 times the market rate, or 12 percent. If the market fell 10 percent, stock **x** fell at 1.2 times 10 percent, or 12 percent. Other stocks always tended to move at less than the market, say, at 0.8 times the market rate. When the market rose 10 percent, stock **y** rose 8 percent; when the market doubled, the stock increased by 80 percent.

This view of a stock's price movements in relation to the market did not say that the 1.2 times rule always prevailed for stock **x**, or that the 0.8 times rule always characterized stock **y**. Rather, this view suggested that these rules held true for the stock on average. Other factors also characterized the situation, including the random movement of the individual stock (what came to be called the unsystematic movement of a stock's price), the random element, and a constant.

We can describe the above model as the Capital Asset Pricing Model (CAPM). Its equation is the following:

$$y = a + bx + z \tag{24.1}$$

where:

y is the price movement of the stock, x is the price movement of the market; a and b are coefficients—a is a constant and b gives the relationship between percentage changes in the stock's price and percentage changes in the market's price; and z is a random variable.

The coefficient b in Equation (24.1) is the beta coefficient. The relationship postulated in Equation (24.1) is a linear one between two rate-of-change variables. The coefficient b, the beta, makes it a multiplicative relationship because one rate-of-change (that of the market) is multiplied by a factor. In the above examples, we used the factors 1.2 and 0.8.

The regression Equation (24.1) is one way to attempt to describe the co-movement of stock prices. When the theory came out, I thought it did not seem a useful description; I was certain that it would disappear. It did not disappear, however. Instead, it became an integral part of the so-called Capital Asset Pricing Model, a theory of stock prices proposed by scholars, taught in business schools, and adopted by some professionals. Like me, most professionals remained skeptical, at least in the early years. Many still do.

Use of a regression equation to forecast changes in an individual stock's price would be extremely useful were the equation developed on one period applicable to the next period. The beta coefficient derived from such an equation also would be useful in measuring the risk involved in owning the stock. Either use depends on how well the regression equation, with its alpha and beta coefficients, describes returns and whether these measures are comparatively stable over time.

To answer the question of reliability, we prepared scatter plots of returns on individual stocks versus returns on the Standard & Poor's 500. Returns were calculated as first differences in the natural logarithms of prices (x100 and rounded to the nearest whole number). The data for the stocks and the Standard & Poor's 500 are given in Chapter 6, Table 6.2. Plots of the first six stocks in the list are given in the six panels in Figure 24.1.

The figure reveals quite clearly that there rarely is a consistent relationship between individual stock returns and returns on the Standard & Poor's 500 Index. Were there significant or useful relationships, the plotted dots would fall along a straight line moving from lower left to upper right. That is not the case; the dots are essentially random. In five of the six stocks, less than one-sixth (R-squared less than 0.16) of the variance in returns is explained by returns on the Standard & Poor's 500. In the sixth stock, only one-third of the variance is explained. Contrary to the theory, market returns in this sample were not very useful in predicting stock returns.

Next, we looked at the alpha and beta coefficients derived from independent periods. Using the data from Table 6.2, we divided the data into two sets: the first covering annual returns between 1982 and 1986, the second covering annual returns between 1987 and 1991. We ran regression equations of five years of returns for the Standard & Poor's 500 against returns for each stock for the 1982–86 period and then for the 1987–91 period. We wanted to determine whether the coefficients for the second period matched the coefficients for the first period. If they did, the coefficients would be useful in predicting stock returns and stock risk. If they did not, then their predictive value would be questionable.

In the first panel of Figure 24.2, alpha coefficients in the first period are plotted against alpha coefficients in the second period. As you can see, the dots do not lie along a straight line. Thus, the relationship between the alphas of the two periods is weak and not signifi-

Figure 24.1 Stocks vs. Market

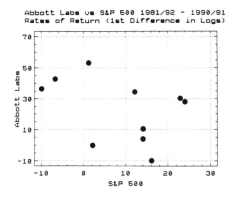

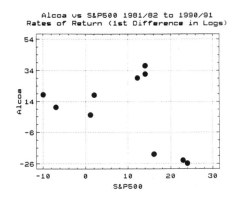

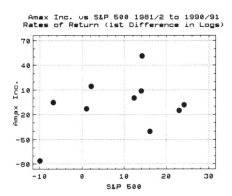

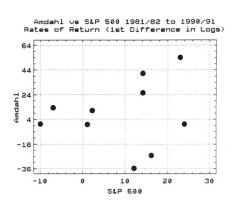

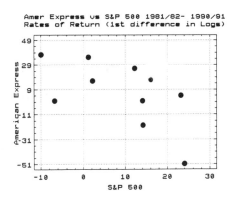

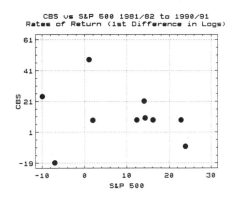

cant. R-squared is 0.04, meaning that only 4 percent of the variance in the alphas was explained by the linear relationship postulated by the theory.

In the second panel of Figure 24.2, beta coefficients in the first period are plotted against beta coefficients in the second. Again, there is little relationship between the two sets of numbers. For the beta, the coefficient of determination (R-squared) is 0.11, which means that only 11 percent of the variance in the betas in the second period is explained by the betas in the first period. In fact, four of the alphas and three of the betas have switched signs.

Evidently, neither alphas nor betas were stable in this time period for this sample of stocks. The data simply appear to be too random to make alphas or betas reliable parameters for estimating an individual stock's return.

Based on this sample of stocks, attempts to run regression lines through returns for individual stocks and returns for the market would have little merit. Perhaps the time sample was too small or the interval of measurement too large. Nonetheless, if the technique were useful we would not have gotten the results we did. On the basis of these tests, regression lines are not useful in estimating returns on individual stocks or in evaluating the risk inherent in them.

What does not work in practice does not make good theory. Recent studies have also shown the lack of significance, first of the alpha and then of the beta coefficients, supporting the evidence given above. We must conclude that a major part of the Capital Asset Pricing Model does not accurately describe the price behavior of individual stocks.

The regression equation also conflicts with the second rule or law (described in Chapter 27), which states that the values of a percentage change variable in one period will not correlate with those of a percentage change variable in another period. The CAPM model implies that firms with high growth rates of stock prices in one period will outperform firms with high growth rates of stock prices in another period, provided the market is up in both periods. Such is not the case.

An alternate model (described in Chapter 6) postulates that the change in the price of a stock is the sum of two random variables: one peculiar to stock, the other peculiar to the market. In this model, the relationship is additive: We add the two random variables to obtain the price change in the stock. The price change in the stock is not a multiplicative function of the market change, the beta, or a function of a constant, the alpha.

The bottom panel of Figure 24.2 shows the relationship between standard deviations in independent periods for the individual stocks. The overall relationship is not very good. However, for half the stocks, the standard deviations in the second period were within 5 percentage points of the standard deviations in the first period. In four of the five cases, the difference was 2 percentage points or less. Three stocks had wide changes in standard deviations. The variability of alphas and betas was much greater than the variability of the standard deviations.

In conclusion, the use of alphas and betas for individual stocks under the Capital Asset Pricing Model is open to question. The standard deviation is a better measure of risk and the Osborne model, described in Chapter 6, represents a more realistic framework for describing the behavior of stock prices.

Figure 24.2   Alpha, Beta, and Standard Deviations in Two Periods

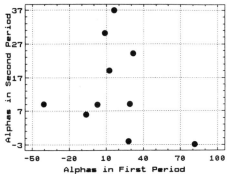

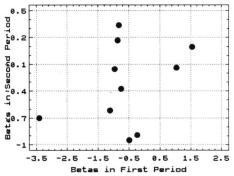

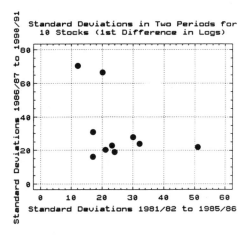

CHAPTER 25

Determining the Probability of Changes in Bond Yields

In past chapters, we have described methods of predicting the probability of changes in a number of different financial variables, ranging from stock prices to profit margins. These methods were based on knowing the standard deviation of the series in question, that the standard deviation rose with the square root of the time interval, and that changes in the logarithms of these variables approximated a normal distribution with a zero mean.

Changes in the logs of interest rates have many of the same characteristics. For that reason, the same techniques that we have applied to other financial series can be applied to interest rates but with several modifications. The principal modification is that the standard deviation of changes in the logs of yields, the volatility of yields so measured, is high for short-term bonds and low for long-term bonds. The relationship is inverse and sufficiently regular to be modeled by an equation; the standard deviation is inversely related to the cube root of the maturity of the bond. Like the distribution of other series, the distribution of changes in the logs of interest rates is approximately normal, of zero mean, and has a standard deviation that rises with the square root of the time-difference interval. Finally, the standard deviation of changes in the logs of interest rates does change from one historical period to another, though the range is generally limited; at the extreme, the range is about 3x between the highest and lowest values of the standard deviation.

The volatility of reported yields increases with the level of the yield, as it must if the volatility of the logs of yields is comparatively stable. This same feature characterizes stock prices. In many respects, we are dealing with the same kind of phenomena as we did with stock prices. We can summarize the principal statistical features of interest rates as follows:

1.   Differences in the logs of interest rates form a random series of zero mean and have an approximately normal distribution and a standard deviation that increases with the square root of time.

2.   The standard deviation of changes in the logs of interest rates is inversely related to the cube root of the maturity of the bond.

3.   However, interest rates themselves and their logs do not form random series. Only differences in the logs of rates are random. The best estimate of the future rate is the past rate.

There are several implications of the above points:

1.   The direction of interest rates cannot be predicted any better than by the flip of a coin.

2.   The probabilities of yield changes over any future period can be determined from the standard deviation and the normal distribution.

The latter two facts enable us to predict the probability of a rise in yields of any given magnitude or, moreover, any future period. Similar statements can be made about a fall in yields, or, as we shall see later, the probabilities of changes in the prices of bonds.

Neither the logs of yields nor the yields themselves are random. The distinctions between these three types of series (i.e., yields, logs of yields, and differences in the logs of yields) is crucial to understanding the pattern and structure of yields. Scholarly papers sometimes ignore this distinction and attempt, for example, to show changes in the volatility of yields, but they fail to determine whether the change in volatility has arisen only because yield levels have risen. The underlying volatility of the first difference in the logs of yields (or the logs of yields) may not have changed at all.

With interest rates, the rise in the standard deviation with increasing time-difference intervals is the same for all maturities, even though the standard deviation is different for different maturities. For instance, bonds of the same maturity in different countries and different historical periods have similar standard deviations. Bonds as remote in time and place from each other as the British counsel in the eighteenth century and the 30-year U.S. government bond, for example, have remarkably similar standard deviations.

The basis for the above conclusion is a study conducted by M. F. M. Osborne and the author in which we considered a variety of yield series, including the Salomon Yield indexes, the Durand Yield indexes, the Macaulay indexes, and other indexes and evidence given in *The Random Character of Interest Rates* (1990). These studies included a variety of tests to determine the presence of randomness in differences in the logs of individual yield series. The result was that every series studied was approximately random and had a zero mean and standard deviation that increased with the square root of time. Not only that, but after taking into account the co-movement of rates among different bond maturities, changes in the logs of the series formed by dividing one yield series by another was also a random series with a zero mean and a dispersion that increased with the square root of time.

The rise of the standard deviation of changes in the logs of the Salomon Brothers three-month U.S. Treasury bill yield index is shown in Appendix VI, along with similar charts for random numbers, stock prices, and other series. This evidence reveals the common features of the different types of series, including random numbers.

We can calculate the standard deviation of annual changes in the logarithms of yields for any particular maturity bond. Since rates for a given maturity bond move together, when we know the standard deviation for that maturity, we know it for any other bond of the same maturity. This assumes, of course, that the credit ratings of the bonds are similar.

Calculating the Probability of a Rise or Fall in Bond Yields

In order to calculate the probability of a rise or fall in bond yields, we must know the one-year standard deviation of changes in the logs of yields for that particular maturity. Table 25.1 gives the one-year standard deviation of changes in the logs of yields but expressed in percent. The table is based on changes in the logs of yields of three-month and 1-, 2-, 5-, 10-, 15-, and 20-year bond yields given in the Salomon Yield Monthly Indexes over the period 1950–1993. A regression equation was fitted to the standard deviations of yield's for various years and maturities, namely:

$$\text{Standard Deviation of Change in Logs of Yields} = 0.28 \times \text{Years}^{0.5} / \text{maturity}^{0.27}$$

If we have a five-year bond and wish to know the standard deviation of changes in the logs of yields, we substitute 3 for the number of years and 5 for the maturity:

$$S = 0.28 \times 3^{0.5} / 5^{0.27}$$
$$= 0.28 \times 1.73 / 1.54$$
$$= 0.28 \times 1.12$$
$$= 0.32$$

The standard deviation of changes in the logs of yields of a five-year bond in three years is 0.32. The antilog of 0.32 is 1.38, or a standard deviation of 38 percent.

Once we know the standard deviation of the particular maturity bond and the current yield, we can use Appendix II to determine the probability of a rise or fall in yields of any percent. For illustration, suppose we have a five-year bond, and the current yield on the bond is 4 percent. We want to know the probability that the yield will rise by 30 percent. That amount of rise would bring the yield on five-year bonds to 4.8 percent a year from now.

The standard deviation of changes in yields of a five-year bond is 20 percent. In Appendix Table IIa, look at the column of standard deviations of 20 percent. Next, look at the left column in that table for the 30 percent rise. Looking across from the 30 percent to the place under a 20 percent standard deviation, we see that the probability of a rise of 30 percent or more is 8 percent. Consequently, there is an 8 percent probability that the yield on a one-year bond will rise by 30 percent or more, or exceed 4.8 percent, a year from

Table 25.1   One-Year Standard Deviation of Various Maturity Bonds

Maturity of Bond in Years	One-Year Standard Deviation of Change in Yield (in percent)
.25	51%
.50	41
1	33
2	27
5	20
10	17
20	14
30	11

now. Appendix Table IIa also shows that the probability of a rise in yields is 50 percent; the probability of a fall is also 50 percent.

If we are interested in changes in yields on one-year bonds two years in advance, we can use Appendix Table IIb, which gives probabilities for two years in the future. The standard deviations for each column are the one-year standard deviations, with the probabilities assigned for two years in the future. For a five-year bond with a 20 percent standard deviation, the probability of a 30 percent rise in yields in the next two years is 15 percent. The procedure to be used in calculating the probability of change in yield is very similar to that used to estimate changes in stock prices, earnings, and profit margins. Probabilities for standards deviations, percentage increases or decreases, and number of years in advance can be interpolated from data in the table.

For longer maturity bonds, the one-year standard deviation declines. For a 10-year bond, the standard deviation is 17 percent and for a 20-year bond, it is 14 percent. For a three-month bill, the one-year standard deviation is 51 percent.

The technique described in this chapter may be used to determine the probability of a rise or fall in interest rates from any current interest rate level for any maturity bond for any forecast period. When the maturity's actual standard deviation is not given in the table, the numbers in the table can be interpolated so that an approximate estimate can be made.

The one-year standard deviations given above as well as the equation are based on U.S. government yields over the period 1950–1993. Other periods will give slightly different standard deviations. Thus, the results of this method are approximate and serve as a guide to probabilities.

CHAPTER 26

How to Read the Probability Tables

The probability tables give probabilities of positive and negative changes for different standard deviations. The standard deviations are given in increments of five, from five to 50. If the standard deviation is not an even multiple of five, simply take the number closest to the one you are interested in. These should cover most of your needs. The probabilities are given for time intervals of from one to 20 years in the future.

The probability tables are given in Appendix II. The tables are based on standard deviations recorded in percents, even though the underlying computation is based on changes in natural logarithms.

In order to use the tables, you first have to determine the standard deviation of the variable you are interested in. Once you have that, you can use the table. Some typical standard deviations are shown in Table 26.1, with the numbers given on an annual basis. You can use these if you haven't calculated precisely the standard deviation you need.

The standard deviation shown in all tables is the one-year standard deviation, though the tables give the probabilities for different numbers of years in the future. Use the one-year standard deviation to find the appropriate column for every table irrespective of the number of years in the future you are interested in.

For example, if you are using a 10 percent standard deviation for one year, you use the same 10 percent for two years or for 20 years since the table has made the adjustment in the probabilities for the increased number of years. You needn't do that yourself as it is all provided for you in the tables.

We will illustrate how to use the tables using Table 26.2 (which has been taken from the more extensive tables in Appendix II).

The procedure is the following:

1. Find the table with the forecast period you want, in this case one year in the future [1].

Table 26.1   Annual Standard Deviation (%)
S&P 425 Industrial Index, 1926–1991

Price	24
Earnings per share	25
Dividends	15
Individual stock price	35
U.S. interest rates 1950–1993	
3-month bill	51
1-year bond	33
5-year bond	20
10-year bond	15
20-year bond	14
Inflation	5

---

2.   Locate the appropriate percent, in this case 15 percent [2]. Use this column to see the probabilities for your standard deviation.

3.   If you are interested in a particular change, locate that. Here we show a 20 percent increase [3].

4.   Find the probability of a change of that much or more, in this case 10 percent. The probability of a 20 percent or greater change one year in the future is 10 percent.

   That's your answer. The probability of a 20 percent or greater increase within the next year for a 15 percent standard deviation is 10 percent.

   Now for the downside risk. It differs from the upside risk because the distribution of price changes is lognormal.

5.   Find the percent decline you're interested in. We'll say 20 percent or more [5].

6.   Look across to the 15 percent standard deviation column. The probability is 6 percent [6] of a 20 percent or greater drop. That is your downside risk.

   If you are interested in four years rather than one, go directly to the four-year table and proceed as we have above. Everything is the same, except that you now have different numbers in the 15 percent standard deviation column and in all other columns as well. In four years the standard deviation is twice as large. It is increased by the square root of four. You look to the 15 percent column in Table IId since we've adjusted the figures in the columns to take account of the increase in years (see Table 26.3). You may think that the probabilities have increased more than they should, even allowing for the rise in years. What has happened is that the normal probability curve doesn't act as you might think it should—a fact that can be seen by looking at the table for the normal curve given elsewhere in this book. The underlying data for the tables is based on natural logarithms.

Table 26.2 (Example of Table IIa) One Year in the Future [1]

Standard Deviation (%)

% Increase/ Decrease	5	10	15[2]	20	25	30	35	40	45	50
Probability of Increase Greater than Shown										
150	0	0	0	0	0	0	0	0	1	1
100	0	0	0	0	0	1	2	3	3	4
90	0	0	0	0	0	1	2	3	4	6
80	0	0	0	0	0	1	3	4	6	7
70	0	0	0	0	1	2	4	6	8	10
60	0	0	0	0	2	4	6	8	10	12
50	0	0	0	1	3	6	9	11	14	16
40	0	0	1	3	7	10	13	16	18	20
30	0	0	3	8	12	16	19	22	24	26
20[3]	0	3	10[4]	16	21	24	27	29	31	33
10	3	16	25	30	33	36	38	39	40	41
0	50	50	50	50	50	50	50	50	50	50
Probability of Decrease Greater than Shown										
0	50	50	50	50	50	50	50	50	50	50
-10	2	13	23	28	32	34	36	38	39	40
-20[5]	0	1	6[6]	11	16	20	23	25	27	29
-30	0	0	1	3	5	9	12	14	17	19
-40	0	0	0	0	1	3	4	6	8	10
-50	0	0	0	0	0	0	1	2	3	4
-60	0	0	0	0	0	0	0	0	1	1
-70	0	0	0	0	0	0	0	0	0	0
-80	0	0	0	0	0	0	0	0	0	0
-90	0	0	0	0	0	0	0	0	0	0

For a 1-year standard deviation of 15 percent, the probability of a 20 percent increase or more at the end of four years is 26 percent. The probability of a 20 percent or more decrease for a 1-year standard deviation of 15 percent after four years is 21 percent.

For data that contain negative figures, you will have to estimate the standard deviation using the figures themselves, which, for example, may be in dollars, or ratios. Once you find the standard deviation, express that as a percent of the latest figure, or whatever figure you are interested in.

Table 26.3   (Example of Table IId) Four Years in the Future

Standard Deviation (%)

% Increase/ Decrease	5	10	15	20	25	30	35	40	45	50
Probability of Increase Greater than Shown										
150	0	0	0	1	2	4	6	9	11	13
100	0	0	1	3	6	9	12	15	18	20
90	0	0	1	4	8	11	14	17	19	21
80	0	0	2	5	9	13	16	19	21	23
70	0	0	3	7	12	16	19	22	24	26
60	0	1	5	10	15	19	22	24	26	28
50	0	2	7	13	18	22	25	27	29	31
40	0	4	11	18	23	26	29	31	33	34
30	0	8	17	24	28	31	33	35	36	37
20	3	17	26	31	34	36	38	39	40	41
10	16	31	37	40	42	43	44	44	45	45
0	50	50	50	50	50	50	50	50	50	50
Probability of Decrease Greater than Shown										
0	50	50	50	50	50	50	50	50	50	50
-10	14	29	35	39	41	42	43	44	44	45
-20	1	12	21	27	31	34	36	37	38	39
-30	0	3	10	16	21	25	28	30	32	33
-40	0	0	3	8	13	17	20	22	25	26
-50	0	0	1	3	6	9	12	15	18	20
-60	0	0	0	1	2	4	6	9	11	13
-70	0	0	0	0	0	1	2	4	5	7
-80	0	0	0	0	0	0	0	1	2	2
-90	0	0	0	0	0	0	0	0	0	0

Say, for example, that the latest earning figure is $10.00 per share and standard deviation of changes in $5.00, presuming you had to use the dollar figures because some of the past earnings were negative. You obviously couldn't calculate percentage changes, or log changes, for deficits.

Now, $5.00 is 50 percent of the latest figure, $10.00. Use the column in the table labeled 50 percent standard deviation. Proceed as above. That's all there is to it.

We could have constructed tables for all kinds of dollar figures, but the above procedure is much easier.

CHAPTER 27

Five Laws of Finance

Some key implications of the random character of stock prices and corporate earnings can be summarized by five rules or laws. The laws permit you to predict the relationship between any two financial variables and to forecast the mean and the variance of the stock market. They are rules of thumb that enable you to evaluate what you hear at a lecture, read in the newspaper or a scholarly article, or are told by you broker, trust officer, or financial adviser. If you are a professional money manager, broker, analyst, student or teacher, the laws will give you a good sense of what to expect in many situations and how to analyze important financial issues. Some of the laws conflict with current theory and practice, and call into question some common methods of analysis and presentation, but they are supported by extensive testing.

The First Law

The first three laws are derived by classifying all financial variables—the numbers you see in *The Wall Street Journal,* in a stock report, or a company annual report—into three types. The three types are: dollar variables; ratio variables; and percentage change variables.

Dollar variables are variables expressed in dollars. They may be original variables, such as net income or total sales of the corporation, or they may be per share figures such as the market price of the stock, earnings per share, or dividends per share. Their common characteristic is that there is a dollar sign before them.

Ratio variables are formed by dividing one dollar variable by another. Good examples are the price/earnings ratio, dividend yield, profit margins (net income/sales), return on equity, and the current ratio. Ratio variables may be recognized by the "%" sign or "x" sign that follows them.

Dollar variables and ratio variables behave in the same way. They change slowly and are comparatively stable. If you know last year's sales for General Motors, for example, you can guess fairly well what sales will be this year or next year. The same holds for its return on equity or price/earnings ratio. Successive dollar, or ratio, variables are dependent on each other. They are not independent.

Table 27.1 provides examples of dollar and ratio variables, and the first law concerns these variables.

If you correlated sales in any industry, say by ranking the firms, you would find a high degree of correlation from one year to the next. Why? Consider sales of firms in the chemical industry: A high degree of order characterizes sales of this industry. Sales of DuPont had been at the top for many years, while sales of Sterling Chemical had been at the bottom of this list. The same consistency of sales was found for companies in other industries. If we correlate sales of companies in one year with sales in the next, the coefficient of correlation will be positive and high. Table 27.2 shows this.

A variety of factors produce this degree of order. A large company, such as DuPont, has a heavy investment in plant, inventory, research and development, patents, and sales and distribution. Its relations with suppliers and customers are extensive and deep. All these factors combine to produce a continuation of a high volume of sales year after year. Sterling Chemical, on the other hand, has resources that are but a fraction of DuPont's. The effect of the disparity is that the large tend to remain large and the small to remain small. Shifts in rank occur slowly and there is a high degree of correlation from one year to the next.

First Law

The values of a dollar or ratio variable of a group of firms in one period will tend to be positively correlated with the values of that same dollar or ratio variable in the next period. The coefficient of correlation will tend to rise as the interval between the periods is decreased.

Extensive tests of the first law are given in Appendix VI.

Table 27.1   Dollar and Ratio Variables

Dollar Variables	Ratio Variables
Sales	Sales/Captial
Operating Income	Net Income/Sales
Pretax Income	Payout Ratio
Net Income	Current Ratio
Dividends	Price/Earnings
Current Assets	Debt/Equity
Total Assets	Equity/Total Assets
Long-Term Debt	
Sales Per Share	
Earnings Per Share	
Price	

Table 27.2   A Ratio or Dollar Variable in Successive Periods

	Sales 1991	Rank	Sales 1992	Rank
DuPont	38.7	1	37.8	1
Dow Chemical	18.9	2	19.0	2
Monsanto	8.9	3	7.8	3
Union Carbide	4.9	4	4.9	4
Arco Chemical	2.8	5	3.1	5
Quantum Chemical	2.5	6	2.4	6
Olin Corp.	2.3	7	2.4	7
Georgia Gulf	.8	8	.8	8
Sterling Chemical	.5	9	.4	9

Sales in $ billions.

The coefficient of correlation was 0.99 (R squared = .99) and was significantly different from zero.

Return on Total Capital (%)

	1991	Rank	1992	Rank
Georgia Gulf	43.6	1	31.0	1
Monsanto	12.5	2	9.2	4
DuPont	8.7	3	10.6	3
Arco Chemical	8.1	4	10.9	2
Dow Chemical	8.0	5	6.8	6
Olin Corp	7.9	6	5.7	7
Quantum Chemical	1.8	7	.6	8
Union Carbide	1.2	8	8.2	5

The coefficient of correlation was 0.95 (R squared = .90) and was significantly different from zero.

The Second Law

Percentage change variables, the third variable, are formed by taking the percentage change in a dollar variable, or a ratio variable. The percentage change in a company's stock price, the percentage change in earnings per share, and the growth of sales are all percentage change variables. Percentage change variables have a "%" sign after them.

Successive values of a percentage change variable are independent; the previous item gives you no idea of what follows.

Table 27.3 provides some examples of percentage change variables.

We can illustrate the second law by the example in Table 27.4, where we show percent changes in earnings per share in two independent periods for seven companies in the chemical industry.

Second Law

The expected coefficient of correlation is zero between the values of a percentage change variable of a group of firms in one period and the values of that same, or any other, percentage change variable in another different period.

Table 27.3   Percent Change Variables

Percent Change in:

Sales	Total Assets
Operating Income	Common Equity
Pretax Income	Earnings Per Share
Earnings	Dividends Per Share
Dividends	Price Per Share

Table 27.4   A Percent Change Variable in Two Periods
Percent Change in Earnings Per Share

	90–91 (%)	Rank	91–92 (%)	Rank
Monsanto	28	1	-42	6
Olin Corp	-18	2	-35	4
DuPont	-24	3	-3	2
Dow Chemical	-30	4	-41	5
Sterling Chemical	-37	5	-88	7
Arco Chemical	-39	6	35	1
Georgia Gulf	-43	7	-33	3

The coefficient of correlation between percentage change in the first period and the percentage change in the second period is negative, low, -0.14 (R squared = .02), and not significantly different from zero.

| Table 27.5 | Return on Total Capital and Change in Earnings Per Share |||||

	Return on Capital 1991 (%)	**Rank**	**Change in Earnings/ Share 1991–92 (%)**	**Rank**
Georgia Gulf	43.6	1	-33	3
Sterling Chemical	21.7	2	-88	7
Monsanto	12.5	3	-42	6
DuPont	8.7	4	-3	2
Arco Chemical	8.1	5	35	1
Dow Chemical	8.0	6	-41	5
Olin Corp	7.9	7	-35	4

The coefficient of correlation was negative, -0.35 (R squared = 0.12) and was not significantly different from zero.

The Third Law

The third law is based on an important difference between dollar and ratio variables, on the one hand, and percentage change variables, on the other: Percentage change variables are random; dollar and ratio variables are not random.

The third law is derived from this distinction. Remember, the first law stated that the coefficient of correlation between values of a dollar or ratio variable in adjacent periods was high and positive. The second law stated that the expected coefficient of correlation between values of a percentage change variable in adjacent periods was zero. If one kind of variable always results in significantly positive correlation and the other kind always results in zero correlation, then we might expect that the first kind of variable would not be related to the second—that the expected correlation between a dollar or ratio variable and a percentage change variable would be zero. That is the essence of the third law.

Table 27.5 illustrates the law. It shows rates of return on total capital, a ratio variable in 1991, and the percentage change in earnings between 1991 and 1992. The results show a correlation not significantly different than zero.

Third Law

The expected coefficient of correlation is zero between the values of a percentage change variable of a group of firms and the values of a dollar or ratio variable of the same firms.

The Fourth Law

In the chapter on the dispersion of changes in stock prices, we showed how the standard deviation of stock prices rises with the square root of time. That relationship may be stated as a law. It applies to any random variable, though it has been tested extensively only on changes in stock prices, interest rates, the Consumer Price Index, and a few other percentage change variables.

Fourth Law

The volatility (standard deviation of changes in the logs of) stocks rises with the square root of time. The same law applies to other financial variables:

$$s(k) = s(1)k^{0.5}$$

The Fifth Law

In a portfolio composed of stocks, each of whose log prices are random and characterized by a lognormal distribution, the mean change will be positive and can be computed from the cross-section standard deviation. There is an upward bias or positive growth. It may be stated as a law.

Fifth Law

When each of the individual stocks in a portfolio has an expected return of zero, and first differences in the prices have a normal distribution, the portfolio itself has a positive expected return. The expected return on the portfolio may be estimated from the standard deviation of first differences in the natural logarithms of the prices of the stocks in the portfolio.

The equation for the fifth law, taken from Chapter 15, is:

$$\text{Mean Change} = \exp(s^2/2)$$

where "s" is the cross-section standard deviation of changes in the logs of prices and under the assumption that the price series is continuous.

From a practical standpoint, there is an important result to this law. The result is that a portfolio of stocks, and market averages, like the Dow Jones Industrial Average or the Standard & Poor's 500, have positive long-term growth. The rate of growth, assuming equal investments in all stocks, depends only on the cross-section standard deviation.

Table 27.6 shows the compound annual growth for various cross-section standard deviations.

As shown in Chapter 15, the cross-section standard deviation of the New Stock Exchange tends to fall somewhere between .30 and .35 resulting in a growth rate of between 4.6 and 6.3 percent per year.

Summary

What do the five laws give us? Above all, some basic knowledge of the whole business of investments, for they provide a way of learning what the expected correlation is between any two financial variables. They tell us which theories are likely to be true and which are likely to be false. The laws also tell us why the risk of the market—or of any other variable like earnings or dividends—rises with time. And they tell us why the market has an underlying built-in growth—and what it is. Thus the five laws, though they may seem somewhat theoretical, have important practical value: They help us to navigate through the choppy seas of conflicting theory and advice that we often receive.

Table 27.6   Expected Annual Growth for Various Cross–Section Standard Deviations

Standard deviation	.10	.15	.20	.25	.30	.35	.40	.45
Compound growth	0.5	1.1	2.0	3.2	4.6	6.3	8.3	10.7

CHAPTER 28

A Summing Up

The goal of this book has been to provide some general concepts that may prove useful in understanding the stock market, and some techniques to use to determine the probability of various outcomes that may be important to your investment decisions.

We have covered some general laws or principles you may use to determine what is occurring. The first three laws classified all financial variables into different types. The first type was expressed in dollar or ratio terms; the second was expressed as a percentage change. The first type tends to be stable, the second random. Dollar and ratio variables are highly correlated from year to year; percentage change variables do not correlate—their past gives little clue to their future. The essence of this distinction is that you cannot predict future growth from past growth. You cannot predict specific future growth from ratios.

The random nature of the stock market brings with it two different, seemingly contradictory, characteristics. Because of randomness, we cannot predict the specific event. We cannot say that Cray Research will rise eight points tomorrow, or that it will be $30 higher at the end of the year. We cannot say that IBM's earnings will rise 10 percent per year each year for the next five years. That kind of predictability is beyond the power of anyone, primarily because there are so many factors that affect future events.

The persistent failure of economists to predict either the direction or magnitude of changes in interest rates any better than the flip of a coin is a well-known illustration of our inability to forecast the specific future event. Their failure is not evidence of lack of knowledge or effort on the part of economists, but simply the intractable nature of the data.

That economists, and others, continue to make such predictions and that highly sophisticated people continue to accept and act on those predictions has always been a cause of wonderment. It probably happens because we have a great need for such information. We accept such forecasts, despite our awareness of their fallibility, because we desire them so much and because decisions must be made. But there are other ways of looking at the future.

If the random nature of the underlying data prohibits us from predicting the specific, at the same time it permits us to make other kinds of predictions—predictions deducible from the very random nature of the data. Most of these predictions result from the inherent characteristics of the distribution of changes in the data, from the fact that changes in the logs of stock prices are random and of zero mean, from the fact that their distribution is normal with a standard deviation that rises with the square root of the time interval over which the change is measured, and from the fact that probabilities may be derived from the normal curve, probabilities that enable us to state that a change will be above or below a certain amount.

This book has attempted to address the practical applications of inherent characteristics of the lognormal distribution. It has focused on the application of the inherent properties in solving practical problems of investment. Just as the inherent properties of the triangle permit the construction of a variety of structures impossible without it, from bridges to office towers, so the lognormal distribution permits estimation of the probability distribution of future values of any variable, estimation of the long-run value of the mean, and calculation of the likely distribution of assets within a common stock portfolio (or the wealth of individuals, or the revenues or profits of corporations), after any interval of time.

Before turning to the applications, we first wish to characterize the distribution. In doing so, we put forth the following principles, or laws:

1. The cross-section correlation between values of a dollar (or ratio) variable in two distinct periods will be positive and high. In other words, the ranking of firms by a particular variable today—like revenues, or market value, or return on equity—provides a good measure of their ranking tomorrow. (First Law)

2. Past values of a random variable—like percent changes in stock prices, company earnings, or mutual fund performance—won't tell you much about future changes. You can predict neither the magnitude nor the specific direction of a growth variable. (Second Law)

3. Future values of a random variable—like earnings growth or stock price changes—won't be related to past or current values of a non-random variable—like price/earnings ratios, dividend payout, or return on equity. (Third Law)

4. The distribution of changes in stock prices and other financial variables is approximately lognormal so that you can predict the future distribution from the past distribution.

5. The standard deviation of first differences in the logs of stock prices and other financial variables rises with the square root of time. (Fourth Law)

6. The expected mean change in a portfolio of stocks, like the Dow Jones Industrial Average, is positive over the long run, even though expected median change is zero. The expected mean change can be calculated from the cross-section standard deviation. (Fifth Law)

7.   The distribution of wealth—common stock assets in a portfolio, the wealth of individuals, or company sales—becomes increasingly skewed with the passage of time.

From these principals, or laws, we can derive a number of useful and practical applications.

The first set of estimations comes directly from the normal distribution. The following examples illustrate the kind of estimates we can make:

1.   We can estimate the probability that a stock price of a particular stock will rise by 10 percent within the next year, or next decade. Or that the price will fall by 10 percent.

2.   We can estimate the distribution of price changes of various magnitudes.

3.   We can determine the probability that a company's profits will rise by 10 percent in the next year, or that they will tumble by half.

4.   We can find the probability that a company now profitable will lose money next year, or three years from now.

5.   We can find the likelihood that a company now in the red will break even next year.

6.   We can estimate the probability of a dividend increase.

7.   We can determine the probability that our return from a mutual fund over the next 10 years will be 10 percent.

8.   We can get a rough estimate of the probability of bankruptcy using the probability of loss as a method of classification, since most companies that go bankrupt are now in red ink, or were.

9.   We can estimate the likelihood that profit margins will double.

All of the above estimates are based on the fact that changes in the logs of the variables are random with a mean of zero, have an approximately normal distribution, and a standard deviation that rises with the square root of time.

We can make a second set of estimates from the antilogs of the normal distribution. The most important of these is an estimate of the distribution of assets within a common stock portfolio after a specific interval of time, a year, a decade. An inevitable result of the random nature of changes in stock prices and the normal distribution is not only that portfolios of common stocks become increasingly undiversified with time, but that we can predict the degree of non-diversification—the skew. The growth of undiversification is an inevitable by-product of the lognormal distribution. For the same underlying reason, the random nature of changes in corporate revenues and incomes, we can estimate the future skewing of corporate shares of the revenue and income markets.

Finally, since the distribution of changes in these economic variables is lognormal we can estimate the long-run mean change, which for the stock market is about 5 percent per year.

These are the things we *can* do. The things we cannot do are to estimate specific rates of growth based simply on past growth, or on ratios. We cannot forecast the returns of a mutual fund based on past returns; we cannot select mutual funds based simply on past returns; we cannot pick the best stock or the best fund in the past and expect it to be the best in the future. There simply isn't enough correlation, or cross-correlation of past and future growth—to do that. There are some departures from this; there is some tendency, not very large, but quite evident, for low price/earnings portfolios to do better than average over the long run than high price/earnings portfolios, in contradiction of the second law. But this tendency is not sufficiently great to contradict the assertion of the principle that there is generally no significant correlation, or little significant correlation, between that ratio and the growth of stock prices.

In conclusion, while it may be heretical to think and propose that all financial variables are random, they are (or seem to be), and that very fact allows us to predict a number of things that are very useful—to an investor, a broker, a corporate official, or anyone else interested in the world of stock prices, corporations, and investments.

APPENDIX I

Questions on Prediction Answered by the First Three Laws

You can use the first three laws, given in chapter 27, to determine whether a given approach is likely to provide a useful prediction. The first seven questions are discussed in detail; the final questions are given in outline form. Most of the questions deal with predicting specific growth rates rather than probabilities. While probabilities can be predicted, as described earlier, specific growth rates are much more difficult to predict.

1. *Can you predict future growth of earnings from past growth of earnings?*

For the vast majority of companies, you cannot, because past and future changes are independent. The percent change next year will bear little relation to the percent last year, or in the last decade.

Even relative future growth cannot be predicted from past growth. The company with the best past growth of earnings, say last year's growth, or the past five year's growth, has only an even chance of being above average next year, or in the next five years.

This independence of past and future growth is contrary to what many people think. It means that continuance of "excellence" when measured by earnings growth is not easy to achieve.

Even though you cannot predict the specific rate of growth, you can predict the probability distribution of future earnings changes. Because the volatility of earnings growth varies from one company to the next, the probability distribution will not be the same for all companies.

2. *Can you predict future growth of the price of a company's stock from past growth? Or, can you predict the future growth of a mutual fund from its past growth?*

The answer here is the same as with growth of earnings. Successive percentage change variables are independent. The past growth of a stock's price, or a mutual fund's, gives little basis for predicting future growth. Lack of correspondence between past and future holds for absolute growth and for relative growth.

Picking the best stock or mutual fund for the future is not easy. You can't simply look at the past growth rate. The extensive records of past mutual fund performance will not help a great deal in choosing the fund with the best future growth. You can see this because the top funds change from year to year, provided you compare performance for independent years.

But stocks and mutual funds do differ in the volatility. You can use differences in volatility to predict the probable distribution of future percentage changes, though not the specific change.

3. *Can you predict future growth on the basis of return on equity, or share of market?*

Again the answer is no. Percentage change variables are independent and highly variable from year to year. Ratios, such as the return on equity or share of market or profit margins, are comparatively stable from year to year. The two different kinds of variables bear little relation to one another.

Consequently, the company with the highest share of market is not necessarily the company that is likely to show the greatest earnings growth. It may not even have much more than an even chance of doing better than average.

The same conclusion may be drawn about other ratios and growth. High return-on-equity companies, high profit-margin firms, will not show better than average earnings growth, or stock price growth, than companies with low returns or low margins. This conclusion violates commonly held views, but the facts support it.

Certainly there are important advantages to high margins, or high return on equity, or high share of market. The advantages include greater ability to pay off debt, remit dividends, finance new activities, and avoid losses or bankruptcy. These advantages should not be minimized. But growth is another matter. The absence of significant correlation between these ratios and growth is due to the comparatively stable behavior of ratios and the much more chaotic behavior of percentage change variables.

4.   *Can you predict future share of market, or profit margins, or return on equity, based on past values of these ratios?*

Yes, you can. Ratios, like share of market, or profit margins, change slowly. You can actually predict the probability that a company's margins, or share of market, or profitability, will change from one level to another. You can make the prediction based on the current level of the ratio, the standard deviation of past changes in the ratio, and the normal distribution, as shown in chapters 12 and 14.

Generally it is difficult to shift relative position with respect to a ratio or a dollar variable. Just because a firm has low margins doesn't mean it is likely to raise them to the industry norm. In fact, the probability of raising margins may be no better than the probability of lowering them. This phenomenon is related to the calculation of long leads and shifts in leads in the probability theory of fluctuations in coin tossing. In both areas, the most likely event is that relative positions won't shift, but the probability of this drops when relative positions are close together, when the volatility of change rises, and, concurrently, when the time interval rises.

5.   *Can you predict relative stock price growth on the basis of price/earnings ratios?*

In general, no. The assertion that you can violates the law that states that the expected correlation between growth variables and a ratio is zero. If you run correlations between price/earnings ratios at the end of one year and growth of price in the next year, or in the next five years, the coefficients generally will not be significantly different than zero. That makes the odds of prediction low.

Notwithstanding the above, if you classify very large numbers of stocks into a few groups by price/earnings ratios and then examine the average price change for each group, you will find a positive correlation with the average price/earnings ratio for each group. The same conclusion applies to the relation between other growth variables, like earnings, or revenues, and ratios.

Doesn't that contradict what we said earlier? Yes and no. It means that for very large groups there is some correlation, but not for individual stocks. There is what we might call weak correlation, which comes out in large aggregations over long periods. The correlation may arise from the tendency of the market to overreact. But for stocks individually, there is generally no significant correlation between future price change and past price/earnings ratios.

6.   *Can you predict future price change if you know future earnings changes?*

Yes. There is a significant positive correlation between earnings changes of stocks and coincident price changes. The longer the period of measurement, the greater the correlation. The tests for this were by groups, not large groups, but relatively small groups. This significant relationship confirms the importance of fundamental factors on stock price changes. It may be and seems to be that a stock's price may be only somewhat related to such things as earnings, but the price does respond to changes in earnings on a relative basis.

7. *Can you predict future corporate problems, such as deficits or bankruptcy, from ratios?*

Yes. Firms with low or negative profit margins have a higher incidence of losses and bankruptcy than firms with high margins, or high returns on assets. In examining this relationship, it is preferable to standardize the ratio by dividing it by its standard deviation, as described in chapter 12. Rarely in the literature or in practice will you find such standardization, but applying it gives you a much better estimate, and an estimate from which you can derive a probability.

***

The following questions show, in outline form but in broader terms, some of the implications of the first three laws. Some questions concern the relation of future changes in a variable to past changes in a variable or to a ratio. Others relate past to future ratios. In all cases where we talk of growth or changes, we refer to absolute growth, to relative growth, or both, unless otherwise specified. Changes refer to percentage changes.

1. Is it possible to forecast future changes in the price of a stock using any of the following?

No it is not.	**Yes it is.**
(from 2nd law)	
Past price change	Concurrent earnings change
Past earnings growth	
Past sales growth	
(from 3rd law)	
Past price/earnings—very slight only	
Past dividend yield	
Past return on equity	
Past dividend payout ratio	

2. *Is it possible to forecast future growth of earnings growth using any of the following?*

No it is not.

(from 2nd law)

Past earnings growth
Past sales growth

(from 3rd law)
> Past return on equity
> Present share of market
> Past or present earnings retention
> ratio—relative to other firms

3.   *Is it possible to forecast mutual fund performance using any of the following?*

No it is not.

(from 2nd law)
> Past mutual fund performance

Using the corresponding past ratios, is it possible to forecast any of the following future ratios?

Yes it is.

(from 1st law)
> Future share of market
> Future return on equity
> Future price/earnings ratio
> Future dividend/yield
> Future profit margins

APPENDIX II

Probability of Various Increases and Decreases for Different Standard Deviations and Various Years in the Future

Table II.a   **1 Year in Future**

Annual Standard Deviation (%)

5	10	15	20	25	30	35	40	45	50

Probability of Increase Greater Than Shown

Increase/ Decrease (%)	5	10	15	20	25	30	35	40	45	50
150	0	0	0	0	0	0	0	0	1	1
100	0	0	0	0	0	0	1	2	3	4
90	0	0	0	0	0	1	2	3	4	6
80	0	0	0	0	0	1	3	4	6	7
70	0	0	0	0	1	2	4	6	8	10
60	0	0	0	0	2	4	6	8	10	12
50	0	0	0	1	3	6	9	11	14	16
40	0	0	1	3	7	10	13	16	18	20
30	0	0	3	8	12	16	19	22	24	26
20	0	3	10	16	21	24	27	29	31	33
10	3	16	25	30	33	36	38	39	40	41
0	50	50	50	50	50	50	50	50	50	50

Probability of Decrease Greater Than Shown

	5	10	15	20	25	30	35	40	45	50
0	50	50	50	50	50	50	50	50	50	50
-10	2	13	23	28	32	34	36	38	39	40
-20	0	1	6	11	16	20	23	25	27	29
-30	0	0	1	3	5	9	12	14	17	19
-40	0	0	0	0	1	3	4	6	8	10
-50	0	0	0	0	0	0	1	2	3	4
-60	0	0	0	0	0	0	0	0	1	1
-70	0	0	0	0	0	0	0	0	0	0
-80	0	0	0	0	0	0	0	0	0	0
-90	0	0	0	0	0	0	0	0	0	0

Table II.b   2 Years in Future

Annual Standard Deviation (%)

	5	10	15	20	25	30	35	40	45	50

Probability of Increase Greater Than Shown

Increase/ Decrease (%)	5	10	15	20	25	30	35	40	45	50
150	0	0	0	0	0	1	2	3	4	6
100	0	0	0	0	1	3	5	7	9	11
90	0	0	0	1	2	4	7	9	11	13
80	0	0	0	1	3	6	8	11	13	15
70	0	0	0	2	5	8	11	13	16	18
60	0	0	1	3	7	10	13	16	19	21
50	0	0	2	6	10	14	17	20	22	24
40	0	1	4	10	14	18	21	24	26	28
30	0	3	9	15	20	24	27	29	31	32
20	0	9	18	24	28	31	33	35	36	38
10	8	24	31	36	38	40	41	42	43	43
0	50	50	50	50	50	50	50	50	50	50

Probability of Decrease Greater Than Shown

	5	10	15	20	25	30	35	40	45	50
0	50	50	50	50	50	50	50	50	50	50
-10	6	22	30	34	37	39	40	41	42	43
-20	0	5	13	19	24	27	30	32	34	35
-30	0	0	4	8	13	17	20	23	25	27
-40	0	0	0	2	5	8	11	14	17	19
-50	0	0	0	0	1	3	5	7	9	11
-60	0	0	0	0	0	1	2	3	4	6
-70	0	0	0	0	0	0	0	1	1	2
-80	0	0	0	0	0	0	0	0	0	0
-90	0	0	0	0	0	0	0	0	0	0

Table II.c   3 Years in Future

Annual Standard Deviation (%)

	5	10	15	20	25	30	35	40	45	50

Probability of Increase Greater Than Shown

Increase/ Decrease (%)	5	10	15	20	25	30	35	40	45	50
150	0	0	0	0	1	2	4	6	8	10
100	0	0	0	1	4	6	9	12	14	16
90	0	0	0	2	5	8	11	14	16	18
80	0	0	1	3	6	10	13	16	18	20
70	0	0	1	5	8	12	15	18	20	22
60	0	0	3	7	11	15	18	21	23	25
50	0	1	5	10	15	19	22	24	26	28
40	0	2	8	14	19	23	26	28	30	32
30	0	6	14	20	25	28	31	33	34	35
20	2	13	23	28	32	34	36	38	39	40
10	13	28	35	38	40	42	43	44	44	45
0	50	50	50	50	50	50	50	50	50	50

Probability of Decrease Greater Than Shown

	5	10	15	20	25	30	35	40	45	50
0	50	50	50	50	50	50	50	50	50	50
-10	11	26	33	37	39	41	42	43	43	44
-20	0	9	18	24	28	31	33	35	36	38
-30	0	2	7	13	18	22	25	27	29	31
-40	0	0	2	5	9	13	16	19	21	23
-50	0	0	0	1	4	6	9	12	14	16
-60	0	0	0	0	1	2	4	6	8	10
-70	0	0	0	0	0	0	1	2	3	4
-80	0	0	0	0	0	0	0	0	1	1
-90	0	0	0	0	0	0	0	0	0	0

Table II.d   4 Years in Future

Annual Standard Deviation (%)

5	10	15	20	25	30	35	40	45	50

Probability of Increase Greater Than Shown

Increase/Decrease (%)	5	10	15	20	25	30	35	40	45	50
150	0	0	0	1	2	4	6	9	11	13
100	0	0	1	3	6	9	12	15	18	20
90	0	0	1	4	8	11	14	17	19	21
80	0	0	2	5	9	13	16	19	21	23
70	0	0	3	7	12	16	19	22	24	26
60	0	1	5	10	15	19	22	24	26	28
50	0	2	7	13	18	22	25	27	29	31
40	0	4	11	18	23	26	29	31	33	34
30	0	8	17	24	28	31	33	35	36	37
20	3	17	26	31	34	36	38	39	40	41
10	16	31	37	40	42	43	44	44	45	45
0	50	50	50	50	50	50	50	50	50	50

Probability of Decrease Greater Than Shown

	5	10	15	20	25	30	35	40	45	50
0	50	50	50	50	50	50	50	50	50	50
-10	14	29	35	39	41	42	43	44	44	45
-20	1	12	21	27	31	34	36	37	38	39
-30	0	3	10	16	21	25	28	30	32	33
-40	0	0	3	8	13	17	20	22	25	26
-50	0	0	1	3	6	9	12	15	18	20
-60	0	0	0	1	2	4	6	9	11	13
-70	0	0	0	0	0	1	2	4	5	7
-80	0	0	0	0	0	0	0	1	2	2
-90	0	0	0	0	0	0	0	0	0	0

Table II.e   **5 Years in Future**

Annual Standard Deviation (%)

	5	10	15	20	25	30	35	40	45	50

Probability of Increase Greater Than Shown

Increase/ Decrease (%)	5	10	15	20	25	30	35	40	45	50
150	0	0	0	1	3	6	9	11	14	16
100	0	0	1	4	8	12	15	18	20	22
90	0	0	2	6	10	14	17	20	22	24
80	0	0	3	7	12	16	19	22	24	26
70	0	1	4	10	14	18	21	24	26	28
60	0	1	7	12	17	21	24	27	29	30
50	0	3	10	16	21	24	27	29	31	33
40	0	6	14	20	25	28	31	33	34	36
30	1	11	20	26	30	33	35	36	38	39
20	5	20	28	33	36	38	39	40	41	42
10	19	33	38	41	42	44	44	45	45	46
0	50	50	50	50	50	50	50	50	50	50

Probability of Decrease Greater Than Shown

	5	10	15	20	25	30	35	40	45	50
0	50	50	50	50	50	50	50	50	50	50
-10	17	31	37	40	42	43	44	44	45	45
-20	2	15	24	29	33	35	37	38	39	40
-30	0	5	13	19	24	27	30	32	33	35
-40	0	1	5	11	15	19	22	25	27	29
-50	0	0	1	4	8	12	15	18	20	22
-60	0	0	0	1	3	6	9	11	14	16
-70	0	0	0	0	1	2	4	5	7	9
-80	0	0	0	0	0	0	1	2	3	4
-90	0	0	0	0	0	0	0	0	0	1

Table II.f   10 Years in Future

Annual Standard Deviation (%)

Probability of Increase Greater Than Shown

Increase/ Decrease (%)	5	10	15	20	25	30	35	40	45	50
150	0	0	2	6	10	13	17	19	22	24
100	0	1	6	11	16	20	23	26	28	29
90	0	2	7	13	18	22	25	27	29	31
80	0	3	9	15	20	24	27	29	31	32
70	0	4	11	18	23	26	29	31	33	34
60	0	6	14	21	25	29	31	33	34	36
50	0	9	18	24	28	31	33	35	37	38
40	1	13	22	28	32	34	36	38	39	40
30	4	19	28	32	36	38	39	40	41	42
20	12	27	34	38	40	41	42	43	44	44
10	27	38	41	43	45	45	46	46	47	47
0	50	50	50	50	50	50	50	50	50	50

Probability of Decrease Greater Than Shown

	5	10	15	20	25	30	35	40	45	50
0	50	50	50	50	50	50	50	50	50	50
-10	25	36	41	43	44	45	46	46	46	47
-20	7	23	31	35	38	39	41	42	42	43
-30	1	12	21	27	31	33	35	37	38	39
-40	0	5	12	19	23	27	30	32	33	35
-50	0	1	6	11	16	20	23	26	28	29
-60	0	0	2	6	10	13	17	19	22	24
-70	0	0	0	2	4	7	10	13	15	17
-80	0	0	0	0	1	3	4	7	9	10
-90	0	0	0	0	0	0	1	2	3	4

Table II.g   15 Years in Future

Annual Standard Deviation (%)

	5	10	15	20	25	30	35	40	45	50

Probability of Increase Greater Than Shown

Increase/ Decrease (%)	5	10	15	20	25	30	35	40	45	50
150	0	1	5	10	14	18	22	24	26	28
100	0	3	10	16	21	25	28	30	32	33
90	0	4	12	18	23	26	29	31	33	34
80	0	6	14	20	25	28	31	33	34	35
70	0	8	16	23	27	30	32	34	36	37
60	1	10	19	25	29	32	34	36	37	38
50	2	14	23	28	32	34	36	38	39	40
40	4	18	27	32	35	37	39	40	41	42
30	12	24	31	36	38	40	41	42	43	43
20	17	31	37	40	42	43	44	44	45	45
10	31	40	43	45	46	46	47	47	47	48
0	50	50	50	50	50	50	50	50	50	50

Probability of Decrease Greater Than Shown

	5	10	15	20	25	30	35	40	45	50
0	50	50	50	50	50	50	50	50	50	50
-10	29	39	42	44	45	46	46	47	47	47
-20	12	27	34	38	40	41	42	43	44	44
-30	3	17	25	31	34	36	38	39	40	41
-40	0	8	17	23	28	31	33	35	36	37
-50	0	3	10	16	21	25	28	30	32	33
-60	0	1	5	10	14	18	22	24	26	28
-70	0	0	1	4	8	12	15	18	20	22
-80	0	0	0	1	3	6	8	11	13	15
-90	0	0	0	0	0	1	2	4	5	7

Table II.h   20 Years in Future

Annual Standard Deviation (%)

	5	10	15	20	25	30	35	40	45	50

Probability of Increase Greater Than Shown

Increase/ Decrease (%)	5	10	15	20	25	30	35	40	45	50
150	0	2	7	13	18	22	25	27	29	31
100	0	5	13	20	24	28	30	32	34	35
90	0	7	15	22	26	29	32	33	35	36
80	0	8	17	24	28	31	33	35	36	37
70	1	11	20	26	30	33	35	36	37	38
60	2	14	23	28	32	34	36	38	39	40
50	3	17	26	31	34	36	38	39	40	41
40	6	21	30	34	37	39	40	41	42	43
30	11	27	34	37	40	41	42	43	44	44
20	20	33	39	41	43	44	45	45	46	46
10	33	41	44	45	46	47	47	47	48	48
0	50	50	50	50	50	50	50	50	50	50

Probability of Decrease Greater Than Shown

	5	10	15	20	25	30	35	40	45	50
0	50	50	50	50	50	50	50	50	50	50
-10	31	40	43	45	46	46	47	47	47	48
-20	15	30	36	39	41	42	43	44	45	45
-30	5	20	28	33	36	38	40	41	42	42
-40	1	12	21	27	30	33	35	37	38	39
-50	0	5	13	20	24	28	30	32	34	35
-60	0	2	7	13	18	22	25	27	29	31
-70	0	0	3	7	11	15	18	21	23	25
-80	0	0	1	2	5	9	12	14	17	19
-90	0	0	0	0	1	2	4	6	8	10

APPENDIX III

Probability of Various Increases and Decreases for Different Standard Deviations and Various Days in the Future

Table III.a   5 Days in Future

Annual Standard Deviation (%)

	5	10	15	20	25	30	35	40	45	50

Probability of Increase Greater Than Shown

Increase/ Decrease (%)	5	10	15	20	25	30	35	40	45	50
15	0	0	0	0	0	0	0	0	0	0
10	0	0	0	0	0	0	0	1	1	2
9	0	0	0	0	0	0	1	1	2	3
8	0	0	0	0	0	1	1	3	4	5
7	0	0	0	0	0	1	3	4	6	8
6	0	0	0	0	1	3	5	7	9	11
5	0	0	0	1	3	6	8	11	13	15
4	0	0	1	3	7	10	13	16	18	20
3	0	0	4	8	13	17	20	23	25	27
2	0	4	11	18	22	26	29	31	32	34
1	4	19	27	32	35	37	39	40	41	42
0	50	50	50	50	50	50	50	50	50	50

Probability of Decrease Greater Than Shown

	5	10	15	20	25	30	35	40	45	50
0	50	50	50	50	50	50	50	50	50	50
-1	4	18	27	32	35	37	39	40	41	42
-2	0	4	11	17	22	26	28	30	32	34
-3	0	0	3	8	12	16	19	22	24	26
-4	0	0	1	3	6	9	12	15	17	19
-5	0	0	0	1	2	5	7	10	12	14
-6	0	0	0	0	1	2	4	6	8	10
-7	0	0	0	0	0	1	2	3	5	6
-8	0	0	0	0	0	0	1	2	3	4
-9	0	0	0	0	0	0	0	1	2	2

Table III.b   10 Days in Future

Annual Standard Deviation (%)

	5	10	15	20	25	30	35	40	45	50

Probability of Increase Greater Than Shown

Increase/ Decrease (%)	5	10	15	20	25	30	35	40	45	50
15	0	0	0	0	0	0	0	1	1	2
10	0	0	0	0	0	1	3	4	6	8
9	0	0	0	0	1	2	4	6	8	10
8	0	0	0	1	2	4	6	8	11	13
7	0	0	0	1	3	6	9	11	14	16
6	0	0	1	3	6	9	12	15	17	19
5	0	0	2	5	9	13	16	19	21	23
4	0	1	4	10	14	18	21	24	26	28
3	0	3	10	16	21	25	28	30	32	33
2	1	10	20	26	30	32	35	36	37	38
1	11	26	33	37	39	41	42	43	44	44
0	50	50	50	50	50	50	50	50	50	50

Probability of Decrease Greater Than Shown

	5	10	15	20	25	30	35	40	45	50
0	50	50	50	50	50	50	50	50	50	50
-1	11	26	33	37	39	41	42	43	44	44
-2	1	10	19	25	29	32	34	36	37	38
-3	0	3	9	16	20	24	27	29	31	32
-4	0	0	4	9	13	17	21	23	25	27
-5	0	0	1	4	8	12	15	18	20	22
-6	0	0	0	2	5	8	11	13	16	18
-7	0	0	0	1	2	5	7	10	12	14
-8	0	0	0	0	1	3	5	7	9	11
-9	0	0	0	0	1	1	3	5	6	8

Table III.c   15 Days in Future

Annual Standard Deviation (%)

	5	10	15	20	25	30	35	40	45	50

Probability of Increase Greater Than Shown

Increase/ Decrease (%)	5	10	15	20	25	30	35	40	45	50
15	0	0	0	0	0	0	1	2	3	4
10	0	0	0	0	2	4	6	8	10	12
9	0	0	0	1	3	5	8	10	13	15
8	0	0	0	2	4	7	10	13	15	17
7	0	0	1	3	7	10	13	16	18	21
6	0	0	2	6	10	14	17	20	22	24
5	0	1	4	9	14	18	21	24	26	28
4	0	2	8	14	19	23	26	28	30	32
3	0	6	15	21	26	29	31	33	35	36
2	2	15	24	30	33	35	37	39	40	40
1	16	30	36	39	41	43	44	44	45	45
0	50	50	50	50	50	50	50	50	50	50

Probability of Decrease Greater Than Shown

	5	10	15	20	25	30	35	40	45	50
0	50	50	50	50	50	50	50	50	50	50
-1	15	30	36	39	41	43	43	44	45	45
-2	2	15	24	29	33	35	37	38	39	40
-3	0	6	14	20	25	28	31	33	34	36
-4	0	2	7	13	18	22	25	27	29	31
-5	0	0	4	8	13	17	20	23	25	27
-6	0	0	1	5	9	12	15	18	21	23
-7	0	0	1	2	5	9	12	14	17	19
-8	0	0	0	1	3	6	9	11	13	16
-9	0	0	0	1	2	4	6	8	11	13

Table III.d   20 Days in Future

Annual Standard Deviation (%)

	5	10	15	20	25	30	35	40	45	50

Probability of Increase Greater Than Shown

Increase/ Decrease (%)	5	10	15	20	25	30	35	40	45	50
15	0	0	0	0	0	1	2	4	5	7
10	0	0	0	1	3	6	9	11	14	16
9	0	0	0	2	5	8	11	14	16	18
8	0	0	1	4	7	11	14	16	19	21
7	0	0	2	6	10	14	17	20	22	24
6	0	0	4	9	13	17	20	23	25	27
5	0	1	7	13	18	21	24	27	29	30
4	0	4	12	18	23	26	29	31	33	34
3	0	9	18	24	29	32	34	35	37	38
2	4	19	27	32	35	37	39	40	41	42
1	19	33	38	41	42	44	44	45	45	46
0	50	50	50	50	50	50	50	50	50	50

Probability of Decrease Greater Than Shown

	5	10	15	20	25	30	35	40	45	50
0	50	50	50	50	50	50	50	50	50	50
-1	19	33	38	41	42	44	44	45	45	46
-2	4	18	27	32	35	37	39	40	41	42
-3	0	9	18	24	28	31	33	35	36	37
-4	0	3	11	17	22	25	28	30	32	33
-5	0	1	6	11	16	20	23	26	28	29
-6	0	0	3	7	12	16	19	22	24	26
-7	0	0	1	4	8	12	15	18	20	22
-8	0	0	1	3	6	9	12	14	17	19
-9	0	0	0	1	4	6	9	12	14	16

Table III.e   30 Days in Future

Annual Standard Deviation (%)

	5	10	15	20	25	30	35	40	45	50

Probability of Increase Greater Than Shown

Increase/ Decrease (%)	5	10	15	20	25	30	35	40	45	50
15	0	0	0	0	1	3	5	7	9	11
10	0	0	1	3	7	10	13	16	19	21
9	0	0	2	5	9	13	16	19	21	23
8	0	0	3	7	11	15	19	21	24	25
7	0	1	5	10	15	18	22	24	26	28
6	0	2	7	13	18	22	25	27	29	31
5	0	4	11	18	22	26	29	31	32	34
4	0	8	16	23	27	30	32	34	36	37
3	2	14	23	29	32	35	37	38	39	40
2	8	23	31	35	38	40	41	42	43	43
1	24	36	40	42	44	45	45	46	46	47
0	50	50	50	50	50	50	50	50	50	50

Probability of Decrease Greater Than Shown

	5	10	15	20	25	30	35	40	45	50
0	50	50	50	50	50	50	50	50	50	50
-1	24	36	40	42	44	45	45	46	46	47
-2	7	23	31	35	38	39	41	42	42	43
-3	1	13	22	28	32	34	36	38	39	40
-4	0	7	15	22	26	29	32	34	35	36
-5	0	3	10	16	21	25	28	30	32	33
-6	0	1	6	12	17	21	24	26	28	30
-7	0	0	4	8	13	17	20	23	25	27
-8	0	0	2	6	10	13	17	19	22	24
-9	0	0	1	4	7	10	14	16	19	21

Table III.f   40 Days in Future

Annual Standard Deviation (%)

	5	10	15	20	25	30	35	40	45	50

Probability of Increase Greater Than Shown

Increase/ Decrease (%)	5	10	15	20	25	30	35	40	45	50
15	0	0	0	1	3	5	8	10	13	15
10	0	0	2	6	10	14	17	20	22	24
9	0	0	3	8	12	16	19	22	24	26
8	0	1	5	10	15	19	22	24	27	28
7	0	2	7	13	18	22	25	27	29	31
6	0	3	10	17	22	25	28	30	32	33
5	0	6	15	21	25	29	31	33	35	36
4	1	11	20	26	30	33	35	36	37	39
3	3	17	26	31	34	37	38	40	41	41
2	11	27	33	37	39	41	42	43	44	44
1	27	38	41	43	45	45	46	46	47	47
0	50	50	50	50	50	50	50	50	50	50

Probability of Decrease Greater Than Shown

	5	10	15	20	25	30	35	40	45	50
0	50	50	50	50	50	50	50	50	50	50
-1	27	38	41	43	45	45	46	46	47	47
-2	11	26	33	37	39	41	42	43	43	44
-3	3	17	26	31	34	36	38	39	40	41
-4	1	10	19	25	29	32	34	36	37	38
-5	0	5	13	20	24	28	30	32	34	35
-6	0	2	9	15	20	24	27	29	31	32
-7	0	1	6	11	16	20	23	26	28	29
-8	0	0	4	8	13	17	20	23	25	27
-9	0	0	2	6	10	14	17	20	22	24

Table III.g   50 Days in Future

Annual Standard Deviation (%)

	5	10	15	20	25	30	35	40	45	50

Probability of Increase Greater Than Shown

Increase/ Decrease (%)	5	10	15	20	25	30	35	40	45	50
15	0	0	0	2	5	8	10	13	15	18
10	0	0	3	8	12	16	20	22	24	26
9	0	1	5	10	15	19	22	24	27	28
8	0	1	7	13	18	21	24	27	29	30
7	0	3	10	16	21	24	27	29	31	33
6	0	5	13	19	24	27	30	32	34	35
5	0	8	17	23	28	31	33	35	36	37
4	1	13	22	28	32	34	36	38	39	40
3	5	20	28	33	36	38	40	41	41	42
2	14	29	35	38	41	42	43	44	44	45
1	29	39	42	44	45	46	46	47	47	47
0	50	50	50	50	50	50	50	50	50	50

Probability of Decrease Greater Than Shown

	5	10	15	20	25	30	35	40	45	50
0	50	50	50	50	50	50	50	50	50	50
-1	29	39	42	44	45	46	46	47	47	47
-2	13	28	35	38	40	42	43	44	44	45
-3	5	19	28	33	36	38	39	40	41	42
-4	1	12	22	27	31	34	36	37	38	39
-5	0	7	16	22	27	30	32	34	35	37
-6	0	4	12	18	23	26	29	31	33	34
-7	0	2	8	14	19	23	26	28	30	31
-8	0	1	5	11	16	20	23	25	27	29
-9	0	0	3	8	13	17	20	22	25	26

Table III.h   60 Days in Future

Annual Standard Deviation (%)

	5	10	15	20	25	30	35	40	45	50

Probability of Increase Greater Than Shown

Increase/ Decrease (%)	5	10	15	20	25	30	35	40	45	50
15	0	0	1	3	6	9	13	15	18	20
10	0	1	5	10	15	19	22	24	26	28
9	0	1	6	12	17	21	24	26	28	30
8	0	2	9	15	20	23	26	29	30	32
7	0	4	12	18	23	26	29	31	33	34
6	0	7	15	22	26	29	32	33	35	36
5	1	10	19	25	29	32	34	36	37	38
4	2	16	24	30	33	36	37	39	40	41
3	7	22	30	34	37	39	40	41	42	43
2	16	30	36	39	41	43	44	44	45	45
1	31	40	43	45	46	46	47	47	47	48
0	50	50	50	50	50	50	50	50	50	50

Probability of Decrease Greater Than Shown

	5	10	15	20	25	30	35	40	45	50
0	50	50	50	50	50	50	50	50	50	50
-1	31	40	43	45	46	46	47	47	47	48
-2	15	30	36	39	41	42	43	44	45	45
-3	6	22	30	34	37	39	40	41	42	43
-4	2	15	24	29	33	35	37	38	39	40
-5	0	9	18	24	29	31	34	35	37	38
-6	0	5	14	20	25	28	31	33	34	35
-7	0	3	10	16	21	25	28	30	32	33
-8	0	2	7	13	18	22	25	27	29	31
-9	0	1	5	10	15	19	22	24	27	28

Table III.i   90 Days in Future

Annual Standard Deviation (%)

	5	10	15	20	25	30	35	40	45	50

Probability of Increase Greater Than Shown

Increase/ Decrease (%)	5	10	15	20	25	30	35	40	45	50
15	0	0	2	6	10	14	17	20	22	24
10	0	2	8	15	19	23	26	28	30	32
9	0	3	11	17	22	25	28	30	32	33
8	0	5	13	20	24	28	30	32	34	35
7	0	8	16	23	27	30	32	34	36	37
6	1	11	20	26	30	33	35	36	38	39
5	2	15	24	29	33	35	37	39	40	40
4	5	20	29	33	36	38	40	41	42	42
3	11	27	34	37	39	41	42	43	44	44
2	21	34	39	41	43	44	45	45	46	46
1	34	42	44	46	46	47	47	48	48	48
0	50	50	50	50	50	50	50	50	50	50

Probability of Decrease Greater Than Shown

	5	10	15	20	25	30	35	40	45	50
0	50	50	50	50	50	50	50	50	50	50
-1	34	42	44	46	46	47	47	48	48	48
-2	20	33	39	41	43	44	45	45	46	46
-3	10	26	33	37	39	41	42	43	43	44
-4	5	19	28	33	36	38	39	40	41	42
-5	2	14	23	29	32	35	37	38	39	40
-6	1	10	19	25	29	32	34	36	37	38
-7	0	6	15	21	26	29	31	33	35	36
-8	0	4	11	18	23	26	29	31	33	34
-9	0	2	9	15	20	23	26	29	30	32

APPENDIX IV

Distribution of Common Stock Assets Among Different Stocks in Subsequent Years for Different Standard Deviations as a Result of the Lognormal Distribution

Table IV.a **Percent in Each Stock**

Annual Standard Deviation 15%
Number of Years Later

Percent in Each Stock

Stock Number	0	1	2	5	10	20	30	40	50
1	11	13	14	16	18	22	25	28	30
2	11	12	13	14	15	17	18	19	19
3	11	12	12	13	13	14	14	14	14
4	11	11	12	12	12	12	11	11	11
5	11	11	11	11	10	10	9	9	9
6	11	11	10	10	9	8	8	7	7
7	11	10	10	9	8	7	6	6	6
8	11	10	9	8	7	6	5	4	4
9	11	9	8	7	6	4	4	3	2

Annual Standard Deviation 20%
Number of Years Later

Percent in Each Stock

Stock Number	0	1	2	5	10	20	30	40	50
1	11	14	15	18	21	26	30	33	37
2	11	13	14	15	16	18	19	20	21
3	11	12	12	13	14	14	14	14	14
4	11	12	12	12	12	11	11	10	10
5	11	11	11	11	10	9	8	8	7
6	11	11	10	10	9	7	6	6	5
7	11	10	10	9	7	6	5	4	4
8	11	9	9	8	6	5	4	3	2
9	11	9	8	6	5	3	2	2	1

Annual Standard Deviation 25%
Number of Years

	0	1	2	5	10	20	30	40	50

Percent in Each Stock

Stock Number									
1	11	15	16	20	24	30	35	39	43
2	11	13	14	16	17	19	20	21	21
3	11	12	13	13	14	14	14	13	13
4	11	12	12	12	11	11	10	9	8
5	11	11	11	10	10	8	7	6	6
6	11	10	10	9	8	6	5	4	4
7	11	10	9	8	7	5	4	3	2
8	11	9	8	7	5	4	3	2	2
9	11	8	7	5	4	2	2	1	1

Annual Standard Deviation 30%
Number of Years Later

	0	1	2	5	10	20	30	40	50

Percent in Each Stock

Stock Number									
1	11	15	17	21	26	34	40	45	49
2	11	14	15	16	18	20	21	22	22
3	11	12	13	14	14	14	13	13	12
4	11	12	12	12	11	10	9	8	7
5	11	11	11	10	9	8	6	5	5
6	11	10	10	9	7	6	4	3	3
7	11	9	9	7	6	4	3	2	2
8	11	9	8	6	5	3	2	1	1
9	11	8	7	5	3	2	1	1	0

Table IV.b **Cumulative Percent**

Annual Standard Deviation 15%
Number of Years Later

Cumulative Percent

Number of Stocks	0	1	2	5	10	20	30	40	50
1	11	13	14	16	18	22	25	28	30
2	22	26	27	30	34	39	43	46	49
3	33	38	39	43	47	53	57	60	63
4	44	49	51	55	59	64	68	71	74
5	56	60	62	65	69	74	78	80	82
6	67	71	72	75	79	83	85	87	89
7	78	81	82	84	87	90	92	93	94
8	89	91	91	93	94	96	96	97	98
9	100	100	100	100	100	100	100	100	100

Annual Standard Deviation 20%
Number of Years Later

Cumulative Percent

Number of Stocks	0	1	2	5	10	20	30	40	50
1	11	14	15	18	21	26	30	33	37
2	22	27	29	33	37	44	49	54	57
3	33	39	41	46	51	58	64	68	71
4	44	50	53	58	63	70	74	78	81
5	56	61	64	68	73	79	83	85	88
6	67	72	74	78	82	86	89	91	93
7	78	82	83	86	89	93	94	95	96
8	89	91	92	94	95	97	98	98	99
9	100	100	100	100	100	100	100	100	100

Annual Standard Deviation 25%
Number of Years Later

	0	1	2	5	10	20	30	40	50

Cumulative Percent

Number of Stocks									
1	11	15	16	20	24	30	35	39	43
2	22	28	30	35	41	49	55	60	64
3	33	40	43	49	55	64	69	74	77
4	44	52	55	60	67	74	79	83	86
5	56	63	65	71	76	83	87	89	91
6	67	73	75	80	84	89	92	94	95
7	78	83	85	88	91	94	96	97	98
8	89	92	93	95	96	98	98	99	99
9	100	100	100	100	100	100	100	100	100

Annual Standard Deviation 30%
Number of Years Later

	0	1	2	5	10	20	30	40	50

Cumulative Percent

Number of Stocks									
1	11	15	17	21	26	34	40	45	49
2	22	29	32	38	45	54	61	66	70
3	33	41	45	51	59	68	74	79	82
4	44	53	56	63	70	78	83	87	90
5	56	64	67	73	79	86	90	92	94
6	67	74	77	82	86	91	94	96	97
7	78	83	86	89	92	96	97	98	99
8	89	92	93	95	97	98	99	99	100
9	100	100	100	100	100	100	100	100	100

APPENDIX V

How to Find the Probability from the Z-Score

In statistics we often show deviations from the mean by measuring them off in units of the standard deviation—often called z-score (or z-value). By using the z-value, we can compare two different distributions. We can also compare values from two different variables. If the distribution is normal, we can tell what proportion of the observations fall above or below or between various values of the variable.

Any value in a distribution can be converted into a z-value by subtracting the mean of the distribution and dividing the difference by the standard deviation. For example, when the mean is 60 and the standard deviation is 10, a raw score of 70 would have a z-value of $(70 - 60)/10 = 10/10 = 1$. That means, 1 standard deviation above the mean = a z-value (or z-score) of 1.

Table V.a   Tables for Finding Probability of Loss from Z-Score

Positive Earnings

Earnings/Standard Deviation of Changes in Earnings (Z-Score)	Probability of Loss (%)
.00	50%
.05	48
.10	46
.15	44
.20	42
.25	40
.30	38
.35	36
.40	34
.50	31
.60	27
.70	24
.80	21
.90	18
1.00	16
1.10	14
1.20	11
1.30	10
1.40	8
1.50	7
1.60	6
1.70	5
1.80	4
1.90	3
2.00	2
2.25	1

Negative Earnings

Earnings/Standard Deviation of Changes in Earnings (Z-Score)	Probability of Loss (%)
.00	50%
.05	52
.10	54
.15	56
.20	58
.25	60
.30	62
.35	64
.40	66
.50	69
.60	73
.70	76
.80	79
.90	82
1.00	84
1.10	86
1.20	88
1.30	90
1.40	92
1.50	93
1.60	95
1.70	96
1.80	96
1.90	97
2.00	98
2.25	99

Table V.b   **Table for Finding Probability of Change in Value**

Change in Value/Standard Deviation of Change (Z-Score)	Probability of Change (%)
.00	50%
.05	48
.10	46
.15	44
.20	42
.25	40
.30	38
.35	36
.40	34
.50	31
.60	27
.70	24
.80	21
.90	18
1.00	16
1.10	14
1.20	11
1.30	10
1.40	8
1.50	7
1.60	6
1.70	5
1.80	4
1.90	3
2.00	2
2.25	1

APPENDIX VI

Testing the First
Three Laws of
Financial Relationships

In order to test the first three laws, Russ Nelson and I ran extensive correlations on dollar, ratio, and percentage change variables for 12 industries. The initial tests were reported in the *Financial Analysts Journal;* later, tests were presented at the annual meeting of the Western Finance Association and in the *Journal of Quantitative and Financial Analysis.*

You will recall that the first law concerned dollar or ratio variables for a group of firms in two periods—cross-sectional correlation.

The First Law

The values of a dollar or ratio variable of a group of firms in one period will tend to be positively correlated with the values of that same dollar or ratio variable in the next period. The coefficient of correlation will tend to rise as the interval between the periods is decreased.

In order to test the first law, we compared dollar and ratio variables for 19 firms in the petroleum industry, 24 companies in the chemical industry, and 22 companies in the metals industry. The data were taken from the Compustat annual industrial tape over the 18 years from 1949 to 1967 for 12 variables. The dollar variables were revenues, pretax income, cash flow, earnings, price, dividends; the ratio variables were price/earnings, dividend yield, earnings/equity, pretax profit margins, common equity/total assets, and dividend payment. To ensure compatibility, only companies that consistently reported on a calendar year basis were included in the sample. All tests on this sample were run using single-year periods; the sample included only companies with a full 18 years of data for all 12 variables.

Because of the large number of coefficients of correlation, over 65,000, we show the frequency distributions of the coefficients for the petroleum industry. Although the tests were restricted to the larger firms of a few industries for selected periods, the consistency of the results suggests that the same results apply to other samples of firms, other length periods, and other years.

The frequency distribution of the 192 coefficients for tests of the first law of the petroleum industry is shown in Table VI.a.

As you can see in the table, all of the coefficients were positive, all were above +.4, and 95 percent were above +.8. Since for this sample, a coefficient of +.44 is significant at the .05 level of significance, all of the coefficients were significantly positive.

Table VI.a	Distribution of Correlation Coefficients of Dollar and Ratio Variables of 19 Petroleum Firms—Adjacent Years								
From	-1.0	-.8	-.6	-.4	-.2	0	.2	.4	.6	.8
To	-.6	-.6	-.4	-.2	0	.2	.4	.6	.8	1.0
Percent	0	0	0	0	0	0	0	1	4	95

The Second Law

The expected coefficient of correlation is zero between the values of a percentage change variable of a group of firms in one period and the values of that same, or any other, percentage change variable in another different period.

The original evidence for the second law was that extensive evidence confirms that changes in stock prices approximate a random walk. The next piece of evidence came from the work on the randomness of changes in earnings. The model of a random walk appears to apply to changes in other financial variables. If changes are random, past changes give no information about future changes. Consequently, a firm's relative growth of any variable in one year will give little clue as to its relative growth in any other year, or to the relative growth of any other variable in any succeeding or preceding year. These characteristics are summarized earlier by the second law.

Note that we have specifically said the lack of relationship applies to variables in different periods, not the same period.

Considerable evidence has been presented in the literature on the lack of correlation of past and future percentage changes of stock prices and earnings per share. This evidence supports the second law for those two variables.

Extensive tests were done on 65 companies in the petroleum, chemical, and metals industries. Based on various combinations of one-year periods, varying lags over the years 1951–1967, and percentage changes in the variables described above, 10,608 coefficients of correlation were computed. The frequency distribution of those coefficients is shown in Table VI.b.

The average coefficient of correlation is approximately zero; 55 percent of the coefficients lie between -.2 and +.2. The proportion that are either significantly positive (greater than +.44) or significantly negative (less than -.44) was approximately 10 percent, the amount that would be expected using a two-tailed test and a level of significance of 5 percent. Similar results were obtained in the chemical and metal industries.

Table VI.b   Distribution of Correlation Coefficients of Pairs of Various Percentage Change Variables in Distinct Periods and for Varying Intervals Between Periods for 19 Firms in the Petroleum Industry

From	-1.0	-.8	-.6	-.4	-.2	0	.2	.4	.6	.8
To	-.6	-.6	-.4	-.2	0	.2	.4	.6	.8	1.0
Number	4	67	623	1,694	3,002	2,878	1,685	563	85	7
Percent	0	1	6	16	28	27	16	5	1	0

The Third Law

The expected coefficient of correlation is zero between the values of a percentage change variable of a group of firms and the values of a dollar or ratio variable of the same firms.

The third law concerns the correlation between a dollar or ratio variable and a percentage change variable.

To investigate the third law in detail, we used the variables described previously. Coefficients of correlation were computed between the values of a percentage change variable and the values of a dollar or ratio variable. Different combinations were examined as were different intervals of time between test years. This resulted in 10,608 coefficients of correlation. The frequency distribution of these coefficients for the petroleum industry is given in Table VI.c.

Table VI.c affirms the hypothesis. The mean coefficient of correlation is approximately zero, and 53 percent of the coefficients fall between -.2 and +.2, or very low. The proportion of coefficients that are significantly positive is significantly negative or roughly 10 percent, the proportion to be expected from a random selection from a population that approaches normality and has a mean coefficient of zero. Similar results were obtained in the study of the chemical and metals industries.

The evidence for the third law, like the evidence for the first two laws, confirms it. The three laws suggest that if you want to estimate future growth, you can't just extrapolate from past growth or from some ratios. The financial world is simply too complex, too complicated, too subject to a wide variety of influences for that. The laws give you guidelines—by remembering them you can generally determine if a relationship between two or more variables may be presumed to exist or not.

Table VI.c	Distribution of Correlation Coefficients of Pairs of Various Dollar or Ratio with Percentage Change Variables for Varying Intervals Between Periods for 19 Firms in the Petroleum Industry								
From	-1.0	-.8	-.6	-.4	-.2	0	.2	.4	.6	.8
To	-.6	-.6	-.4	-.2	0	.2	.4	.6	.8	1.0
Number	1	132	558	1,469	2,684	3,018	1,970	680	55	0
Percent	0	1	5	14	25	28	19	6	1	0

APPENDIX VII

The Effect of the Holding Period, or Time, on Dispersion

One of the most important characteristics of a random series is that the dispersion of the series rises with the square root of time. If we take the standard deviation as our measure of dispersion, we will find that it rises with the square root of the holding period, or with time. The standard deviation is a general measure of volatility, and as such its tendency to rise with the square root of time reveals that volatility rises with time.

To cite specific examples, the degree of change in changes in stock prices, measured by the standard deviation, rises with the square root of the holding period. We can show this by the following example. In this example, the standard deviation of annual changes in stock prices is 18 percent. To obtain the standard deviation of changes for any other number of years, we multiply the one-year standard deviation by the square root of the number of years.

Standard deviation for n years

$$= 1\text{-year standard deviation} \times (\text{number of years})^{0.5}$$

Taking the one-year standard deviation as 18 percent, we obtain the following figures for standard deviations for from two to 10 years:

Number of Years	Years$^{0.5}$ $\times$ 18% =				Standard Deviation for n years
1	1	$\times$	18%	=	18%
2	1.41	$\times$	18	=	25
3	1.73	$\times$	18	=	31
4	2	$\times$	18	=	36
5	2.24	$\times$	18	=	40
6	2.45	$\times$	18	=	44
7	2.65	$\times$	18	=	48
8	2.83	$\times$	18	=	51
9	3	$\times$	18	=	54
10	3.16	$\times$	18	=	57

If you know the standard deviation for one-year changes in stock prices, or say in the Dow Jones Industrial Average, you can calculate the standard deviation for any other number of years using the above formula. The formula is not perfect—it is approximate, but it is sufficiently accurate to be useful.

When we plot a relationship, such as the square-root rule shown above, on log-log paper, we get a straight line with a slope of one-half. The one half corresponds to the $t^{.5}$ rule. The rise in the standard deviation is always half the run; the change in the value of the change in y is exactly half the value of the change in x. We can show that in the first panel of Figure VII, which gives the standard deviation versus the time interval for the data given above. This plot and all the others are on a log-log scale.

The first panel of Figure VII is an ideal figure in which the relationship is perfect. In practice we will obtain only an approximate figure. The slope, rather than being 0.5, may range as high as 0.6 or as low as 0.4, or even wider afield, and the dots will not lie on a perfectly straight line. To show the degree of approximation, we show figures for selected random, stock market, corporate earnings and revenues, consumer price index, and interest rate data. In each case, we use overlapping intervals, which tend to smooth the data somewhat. For both overlapping and nonoverlapping data, the fit of a regression line is significant at the 5 percent level of significance, which means that the relationship is not due to chance, but real.

The second panel of Figure VII is for a set of random data. You can see that the slope is very close to one-half, the square root rule. The actual slope is 0.5.

The third panel of Figure VII gives the standard deviation of changes in the natural logarithm of stock prices versus the differencing interval. The data is for the Standard & Poor's 500 index for the years 1926–1985. You can see that the slope is 0.5. More extensive examples are given in Osborne (1957), who provides data both for sequential data and cross-sectional data. Both kinds of data have a slope of approximately 0.5.

The fourth panel of Figure VII is for earnings of the Standard & Poor's 500 over the same period. The y-axis gives the standard deviation of changes in the natural logarithm of earnings and the x-axis gives the time (difference) interval. The slope is slightly more than 0.5.

The fifth panel covers Standard & Poor's 500 Dividends, the standard deviation of changes in the natural logarithm of dividends on the y-axis versus the difference interval on the x-axis. Again, you can see that the slope is 0.5 indicating a rise in the standard deviation with the square root of time.

The sixth panel of Figure VII covers yields on the Salomon Brothers 3-Month U.S. Treasury bill yield index for the period 1950–1986. It shows the standard deviation of changes in the logs of yields versus the time difference interval. Again you can see how the standard deviation rises with the square root of time—a slope of 0.5.

The above figures covered five different economic series and for each the standard deviation of changes in the logs of the series increased approximately with the differencing, or holding, interval, or with time. The significance of this mathematical relationship is that if we know the standard deviation for one holding period, we can estimate the standard deviation for other holding periods. We can forecast, for any interval, within certain bounds, the standard deviation of changes in stock prices, or corporate earnings, or the consumer price index. The forecast should be made in the same way we calculated the standard deviation in the example at the beginning of the chapter.

Once we know the standard deviation and once we know that the distribution of changes reflects a well-known distribution, like the normal distribution, then we can forecast the probability of a change greater than, or less than, any magnitude. We have the power to make forecasts of probability distributions.

That's the practical use. The theoretical significance of the previous demonstration of the square-root rule is that it is evidence of the random nature of changes in the previous economic series. In a random series, dispersion, measured by the standard deviation,

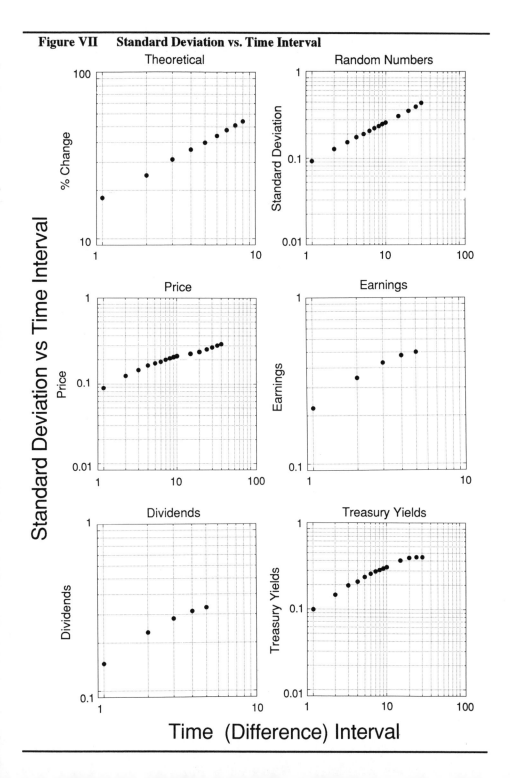

increases with the square root of time. In a non-random series that is not the case. The fact that each of the above series has a standard deviation that increases with the square root of time is evidence that they behave like a random series, like a random walk. That being the case, we have evidence for the application of the structure of random series to making statements about the future, forecasts, about stock prices, earnings, and other investment variables.

APPENDIX VIII

Formulas

Let $x_{j,t}$ represent the value of a dollar or ratio variable for the j_{th} firm ($j = 1,2,...,n$) at time t ($t = 1,2,...,n$). Furthermore, let

$$X_t = [x_{1,t}, x_{2,t}, \ldots, x_{n,t}] \text{ and}$$
$$X_{t+k} = [x_{1,t+k}, x_{2,t+k}, \ldots, x_{n,t+k}]$$

where X_t represents the values of a dollar or ratio variable for m firms at time t and X_{t+k} represents the values of this same variable for the same group of firms at time t+k. To illustrate, X_t might represent earnings of firms in the chemical industry in 1986 and X_{t+k} might represent earnings of the same firms in 1987. The first law states:

$$E \text{ cor } (X_t, X_{t+k}) \rightarrow 1 \text{ as } K \rightarrow 0 \tag{1}$$

where "E cor" stands for the expected coefficient of correlation. The first law states that the expected value of the coefficient of correlation between X_t and X_{t+k} tends to 1 as k tends to 0. As the value of k departs from zero, the absolute value of the coefficient may be expected to decline from 1.

Next, let

$$\Delta x_{j,t} = 100 (x_{j,t} - x_{j,t-k}) / x_{j,t-k}$$

where $\Delta x_{j,t}$ represents the percentage change in a dollar or ratio variable of the j_{th} firm between period t–k and period t.

Furthermore, let

$$\Delta X_t = [x_{1,t}, x_{2,t}, \ldots, x_{n,t}] \text{ and}$$
$$\Delta Y_{t+k} = [Y_{1,t+k}, Y_{2,t+k}, \ldots, Y_{n,t+k}]$$

where ΔX_t represents the values of a percentage change variable in period t, and ΔY_{t+k} represents the values of the same, or a different, percentage change variable in period t+k. For example, ΔX_t and ΔY_{t+k} might represent percentage changes in sales of firms in the chemical industry in 1986 and 1987, respectively.

Then, the second law states:

$$E \text{ cor } (\Delta X_t, \Delta Y_{t+k}) = 0 \tag{2}$$

where $k \neq 0$ and $X = Y$ or $X \neq Y$

Equation (2) states that the expected coefficient of correlation is zero between a percentage change variable (ΔX_t) in one period and the same, or any other, percentage change variable (ΔY_{t+k}) in another different period. From Equations (1) and (2), it is possible to infer a third law, namely:

$$E \, cor \, (X_t, \Delta Y_{t+k}) = 0 \ \text{where} \ X = Y \ \text{or} \ X \neq Y \tag{3}$$

where k may or may not equal zero and X_t and ΔY_{t+k} may or may not be the same variable.

Equation (3) states that the expected coefficient of correlation between a dollar or ratio variable (X_t) and a percentage change variable (ΔY_{t+k}) is zero.

We have defined a percentage change variable as $100 \, (y_t - y_{t-k}) \, / \, y_{t-k})$. The equations apply equally well if we use—instead of the percentage change—the first difference in the natural logarithms, i.e., $\ln(y_t) - \ln(y_{t-k})$. For changes of under 15 percent, the first difference in the natural logs is nearly the same as the percentage change, i.e., a percentage change of 10 percent is the same as the difference in the natural logs of 0.10.

If first differences in the natural logarithms are approximately normally distributed, with a standard deviation σ, and if σ is approximately stable over time, then it is a fact that σ will increase with the square root of time. Letting σ represent the standard deviation and

$$u_t = \ln(y_t) - \ln(y_{t-k})$$

over the time interval k, then

$$\sigma_k = \sigma_1 \, k^{0.5} \tag{4}$$

Equation (4) means that if the standard deviation in one year is σ, then the standard deviation in k years will be the square root of k times σ. This property of random variates has been demonstrated for log differences in stock prices, earnings, and interest rates.

The expected mean of a lognormal variate is given by Aitchison and Brown [1957]:

$$E \, avg \, exp \, (u) = exp \, (avg \, (u) + \sigma^2 / 2)$$

If the expected change in the natural logarithms of prices is zero:

$$E \, avg \, u_t = 0$$

Then, the expected change in the antilog is:

$$E \, avg \, exp \, (u) = exp \, (\sigma^2 / 2) \tag{5}$$

The variance of exp(u) is given by:

$$E \, \sigma^2 \, exp \, (u) = exp \, (4\sigma^2 / 2) \tag{6}$$

The probability density function is given by:

$$Y = (1/\sqrt{2\pi})\exp^{-0.5\,(u-\mu)/\sigma} \qquad (7)$$

APPENDIX IX

Notes to Chapters

Chapter 1—Overview

Strictly speaking, one doesn't predict probabilities; one estimates probabilities from relative frequencies of occurrence in the past. One assumes stationarity, i.e., time independence of probabilities, and hence that the same probabilities hold for the future. This is frequently not the case. The size of the probability and the circumstances under which you use it can make a big difference. If the probability of rain (or a deficit) is 40 percent, but you estimate 30 percent, that's not a big difference practically speaking. In other circumstances (death, accidents, disease, default on debt, failure of a part) this difference (in insurance rates or risk aversion) between a 1 percent, versus 5 percent or 10 percent, probability of occurrence can make a great deal of difference. Witness the experience of banks with loans.

Chapter 2—The Standard Deviation, the Normal Distribution and Natural Logarithms—Concepts Useful for Studying the Stock Market

The lognormal distribution is discussed more fully in Chapter 3.

Chapter 3—The Statistical Basis for Estimating Future Probable Changes in Stock

A detailed description of the lognormal distribution of stock prices may be found in Osborne, M.F.M., "Brownian Motion in the Stock Market," *Operations Research,* 7 (1959), 145–173. Other financial variables, such as corporate earnings or interest rates, have the same statistical characteristics. See notes to Chapter 5.

Chapter 4—How Knowing the Probability Can Improve Your Investment Decisions

The illustrations in this chapter are fictional, though they are based on real life examples.

Illustrations of the use of probability for investment decisions are given in Murphy, J.E., *With Interest: How to Profit from Interest Rate Fluctuations.* 1986. Dow Jones–Irwin, Homewood, Illinois.

Chapter 5—The Dispersion of Stock Prices

I measure dispersion by the standard deviation of changes in the logarithms of prices.

The assumption that transactions take place evenly in time is not true. Volume is much higher today than it was a decade or two ago. Yet, the square-root rule does describe the relationship approximately. The stability of the standard deviation is discussed in Chapter 9.

The terminology on the "square root of time rule" is the following. If we compute differences in the logs of a price series, the standard deviation of those log price changes rises with the square root of the differencing interval. I also call that differencing interval by the terms "time" and "holding period." In the terminology of a random walk, it is called the step length. In the terminology of fluctuations of coin tossing, it's the number of flips of the coin. All these terms designate the same general phenomena.

That the rule characterizes random walks, or random variables, is well known and can be found in books on statistics and articles on Brownian Motion.

The evidence for the rule in the stock market is given in Osborne, M.F.M., "Brownian Motion in the Stock Market," *Operations Research,* 7 (1959), 145–173. Evidence for the rule in earnings appears in Osborne, M.F.M. and Murphy, J.E., "Financial Analogs of Physical Brownian Motion, as Illustrated by Earnings," *The Financial Review,* 19 (1984), 153–172.

The formula for computing the difference in the logs of price is:

$$\Delta x \, (\, k \,) \; = \; \log_e p \, (\, t + k \,) \, / \, p \, (\, t \,) \, , \text{ or equivalently}$$

$$\Delta x \, (\, k \,) \; = \; \log_e \, p \, (\, t + k \,) \; - \; \log_e \, p \, (\, t \,)$$

In this formula, k is the differencing interval, or time. The standard deviation of x(k) rises with the square root of k, or with $k^{0.5}$. The variable $\Delta x(k)$ is also the percentage change in p (or price) between times t and t+k, using continuous compounding.

In Table 5.2 the mean and median is not included.

Chapter 6—The Basic Model of the Stock Market

I believe that Osborne was the first person to propose the model described here based on a lognormal distribution; subsequently others have put forth similar models. Osborne examined the relationship between what he called the differencing interval and the standard deviation, $s(t) = s(1) \times t^{0.5}$; he used that relationship to demonstrate Brownian Motion in the market. He also pointed out that the lognormal distribution of changes in prices would result in an annual increase in the market of about 5 percent per year (see Chapter 15). Surprisingly, this important characteristic is seldom recognized in the literature, despite the fact that it is largely responsible for the market's long-term growth.

The nature of the distribution of changes in stock prices has been the result of considerable study and debate; that the distribution is approximately normal, there is no question. The Student or t distribution approximates the normal for large n. Praetz argues that the Student distribution is a better approximation of stock prices; Mandelbrot reports that monthly prices are stable Paretian while the averages seem to be normal. It should be noted that the sums of random variables approach the normal with increasing time. For other work on the subject see the following:

Blattberg, Robert C. and Gonedes, Nicholas J., "A Comparison of the Stable and Student Distributions as Statistical Models for Stock Prices," *Journal of Business*, 47 (April 1974), 244–280.

Blattberg, Robert C. and Gonedes, Nicholas J., "A Comparison of the Stable and Student Distributions as Statistical Models for Stock Prices: Reply," *Journal of Business*, 50 (January 1977), 78–79.

Mandelbrot, B., "The Variation of Certain Speculative Prices," *Journal of Business*, 36 (October 1963), 394–419.

Mandelbrot, B., "The Variation of Some Other Speculative Prices," *Journal of Business*, 40 (October 1967), 393–413.

Mandelbrot, B. and Fama, E. F., "The Behavior of Stock Market Prices," *Journal of Business*, 38 (January 1965), 34–105.

Mandelbrot, B. and Taylor, H. M., "On the Distribution of Stock Price Differences," *Operations Research*, 15 (1967), 1057–1062.

Osborne, M.F.M., "Brownian Motion in the Stock Market," *Operations Research*, 7 (1959), 145–173.

Osborne, M.F.M., *The Stock Market and Finance from a Physicist's Viewpoint*, published by the author (1977), 3803 24th Avenue, Temple Hills, MD, 20748.

Praetz, Peter D., "The Distribution of Share Price Changes," *Journal of Business*, 45 (January 1972), 49–55.

Praetz, Peter D., "A Comparison of the Stable and Student Distributions as Statistical Models for Stock Prices: Comment," *Journal of Business*, 50 (January 1977), 76–77.

Chapter 8—How to Reduce Common Stock Portfolio Risk

The literature on this topic is very large, particularly theoretical articles. Latane describes the theoretical model for the effect of the number of securities on nonmarket risk and shows how the model applies to the Fisher Lorie data. Other writers have reached similar conclusions. Latane, Henry A., "Cross-Section Regularities in Returns in Investments in Common Stocks," *Journal of Business*, 46 (October 1973), 512–517.

Blume, Marshall E., "On the Assessment of Risk," *Journal of Finance*, 27 (March 1971), 1–10.

Brennan, Michael J., "The Optimal Number of Securities in a Risky Asset Portfolio When There are Fixed Costs of Transaction: Theory and Some Empirical Results," *Journal of Financial and Quantitative Analysis*, 10 (September 1975), 483–496.

Elton, Edwin J. and Gruber, Martin, J., "Risk Reduction and Portfolio Size: An Analytical Solution," *Journal of Business*, 50 (October 1977), 415–437.

Evans, John L. and Archer, Stephen H. "Diversification and the Reduction of Dispersion: An Empirical Analysis," *Journal of Finance,* 23 (December 1966), 761–67.

Jennings, Edward, "An Empirical Analysis of Some Aspects of Common Stock Diversification, " *Journal of Financial and Quantitative Analysis,* 6 (March 1971), 797–813.

Johnson, A. and Shannon, B., "A Note on the Diversification and Reduction of Risk," *Journal of Financial Economics,* 1 (1974), 365–72.

Markowitz, Harry, *Portfolio Selection,* New York, Wiley, 1959.

Markowitz, Harry, "Markowitz Revisited," *Financial Analysts Journal,* 32 (September–October 1976), 47–52.

Wagner, W. and Lau, S., "The Effect of Diversification on Risk," *Financial Analysts Journal,* 27 (November–December 1971), 48–53.

Whitmore, G. A., "Diversification and the Reduction of Dispersion: A Note," *Journal of Financial and Quantitative Analysis,* 5 (June 1970), 263–264.

Chapter 9—Are There Changes in Stock Market Volatility?

R.R. Officer demonstrated in 1973 that the stock market over the period 1897–1926 was not stationary; it was much more volatile at the time of the Great Depression than in prior or subsequent periods. Officer used a running 12-month standard deviation of monthly returns, though the precise definition of how he computed the returns is not clear.

Boness, A. A. Chen and S. Jatusipitak, "Investigation of Nonstationarity in Prices," *Journal of Business,* 47 (October 1974), 518–537.

Officer, R. R., "The Variability of the Market Factor of the New York Stock Exchange," *Journal of Business,* 46 (July 1973), 434–453.

See also Schwert, G. William, "Indexes of U.S. Stock Prices from 1802 to 1987," *Journal of Business,* 63 (March 1990), 399–426.

Chapter 10—Predicting Probable Returns from a Single Stock

The estimated probability distribution of returns excludes both the dividend and an estimate of the mean change. The probability distribution can be adjusted to include these elements.

Chapter 11—Estimating Probable Returns on a Mutual Fund

It would be better to calculate the standard deviation using the change in logarithms of prices. In calculating probable returns, I've ignored the 6.8 percent mean increase in price. Whether this should be set at zero, as I've done, or not, is a matter of debate.

Sharpe, William F., "Mutual Fund Performance," *Journal of Business* 39 (January 1966), 119–138.

Chapter 12—Predicting the Probability of Loss

Murphy, J.E. and Osborne, M.F.M., "Games of Chance and the Probability of Corporate Profit or Loss," *Financial Management,* 8:2 (Summer 1979), 82–88.

Chapter 13—Predicting Probable Changes in Earnings

The distribution of changes in earnings of individual corporations is approximately lognormal with a standard deviation that increases approximately with the square root of time.

Chapter 14—Predicting Probable Changes in Profit Margins

Although the example is fictional, the practice of anticipating an improvement in considering or making acquisitions is common.

Chapter 15—How to Estimate the Average Future Return from Stocks

The fact that the expected mean return on the market is greater than zero even though the expected change in the logs of stock prices is zero was first pointed out by M.F.M. Osborne in his article, "Brownian Motion in the Stock Market," *Operations Research,* 7 (1959), 145–173. The formula for calculating the expected growth in the mean from the cross-section standard deviation of changes in the logs was suggested to me by Tim Cohn of the U.S. Geological Survey. The formula assumes a lognormal distribution of a continuous series.

The percentage change quartiles used to compute the standard deviations in Table 15.2 were adopted with permission, from McEnally, R. W. and Todd, R. B., "Cross-Sectional Variation in Common Stock Returns," *Financial Analysts Journal* (May-June 1992), 77–78, Table I. Though the authors measured the variability of percentage changes in prices, it is better to measure the variability of changes in the logs of prices since the distribution of stock price changes is lognormal.

Chapter 16—The Law of the Distribution of Wealth

Fisher, Lawrence and Lorie, James H., "Some Studies of Variability of Returns on Investments in Common Stocks," *Journal of Business,* 43 (April 1970), 99–134.

Chapter 17—Diversification Across Time

The idea of this chapter was suggested by Dick Jensen of First Asset Management, Minneapolis. The data from which the tables in the original edition were derived contained errors; the underlying data and resulting tables have been corrected in this edition.

Chapter 18—Predicting Dividend Changes

Murphy, J.E. and Johnson, R.S. "Predicting Dividend Changes," *Trusts & Estates* (August 1972), 638–641.

Chapter 19—The Basis for Predicting the Probability of Loss

In view of the high correlation between negative income, or deficits, and bankruptcy, the statistical properties of changes in earnings, and the ability to project the probability distribution of those changes, it is more useful, I believe, to use the conceptual framework of this chapter for forecasting the probability of bankruptcy, or discontinuance. We found that the probability of loss correlated very well with the incidence of bankruptcy on both an *ex anti* and *ex post* basis. I think this is preferable to the use of ratios or discriminant analysis.

Murphy, J.E. and Osborne, M.F.M., "Games of Chance and the Probability of Corporate Profit or Loss," *Financial Management,* 8:2 (Summer 1979), 82–88.

Osborne, M.F.M. and Murphy, J.E., "Financial Analogs of Physical Brownian Motion, as Illustrated by Earnings," *The Financial Review,* 19:2 (1984), 153–172.

Chapter 20—The Importance of Dividends

The rates of return are taken from Ibbotson, R. G. and Brinson, G. P., *Investment Markets,* McGraw-Hill, New York, 1986, Table 5.6, p. 77. Dividend returns were computed by taking the difference between total returns and capital appreciation. For a discussion of the indexes, see Schwert, G. William, "Indexes of U.S. Stock Prices from 1802 to 1987," *Journal of Business,* 63 (March 1990), 399–426.

Chapter 21—Estimating the Standard Deviation from High and Low Stock Prices

Parkinson describes the high/low method in terms of the variance of price, which he calls the diffusion constant that characterizes a random walk. The variance of the variance is five times as large for the closing price method as it is for the high/low price method. Parkinson tested his results using a set of random numbers.

Feller, W., "The Asymptomatic Distribution of the Range of Sums of Random Variables," *Annals of Mathematical Statistics,* 22 (1951), 427–32.

Garman, M. B. and Klass, M. J., "On the Estimation of Security Price Volatilities from Historical Data," *Journal of Business,* 53:1 (January 1980), 67–78.

Parkinson, M., "The Extreme Value Method for Estimating the Variance of the Rate of Return," *The Journal of Business,* 53:1 (January 1980), 61–78.

Chapter 22—Rescaled Range (R/S) Analysis

The R/S versus n statistics were computed using the method described. For further references see:

Ambrose, Brent W., Ancel, Esther W., and Griffiths, Mark D., "Fractal Structure in the Capital Markets Revisited," *Financial Analysts Journal,* 49 (June 1993), 73–77.

Feder, Jens, *Fractals,* Plenum Press, New York, 1988.

Peters, Edgar E., *Chaos and Order in the Capital Markets: A New View of Cycles, Prices, and Market Volatility,* John Wiley & Sons, Inc., New York, 1991.

Peters, Edgar E., "Fractal Structure in the Capital Markets," *Financial Analysts Journal,* 45 (July-August 1989), 32–37.

Peters, Edgar E., "R/S Analysis Using Logarithmic Returns," *Financial Analysts Journal,* 48 (November-December 1992), 81–82.

Chapter 23 —Options : Estimating Probable Price Changes in Evaluating Options

For a description of options, I am indebted to the following book: Robert W. Kolb, *Options: The Investor's Complete Toolkit,* New York Institute of Finance, New York, 1991. The material on the probability of price changes was not taken from that book.

Chapter 24—Betas Don't Work Very Well for Individual Stocks

Guerard, John and Vaught, H. T., *The Handbook of Financial Modeling,* Probus Publishing Company, Chicago, 1989, 221–224.

Ross, Stephen A., "Is Beta Useful?" *The CAPM Controversy,* AIMR, Charlottesville, VA, 1993, 11–15. Ross says, "...the empirical truth is that no systematic relationship can be discerned between expected return and beta." *Ibid.,* 11.

Sharpe, William F., *Investments,* 3rd. ed., Prentice Hall, New York, 1985, 168–169. Sharpe says: "A security's beta value measures the expected change in its return per 1% change in the return on the market portfolio."

Chapter 25—Determining the Probability of Changes in Bond Yields

The standard deviations are based on equations derived from the Salomon monthly yield indexes, 1950–1993. Salomon Brothers, *Analytical Record of Yields and Yield Spreads from 1945,* New York, January 1993. The method used is described in Murphy, J. E. and Osborne, M.F.M., "Predicting the Volatility of Interest Rates," *Journal of Portfolio Management* (Winter 1985), 66–69.

Standard deviations of changes in the logs of yields for a particular maturity for time difference intervals from 1 to n months were regressed against the logs of n. Alternately, multiple regression coefficients were computed for standard deviations for a matrix of difference intervals and bond maturities.

The evidence for randomness in bond yields is given in the following:

Murphy, J. E. and Osborne, M.F.M., "Brownian Motion in the Bond Market," *The Review of Futures Markets,* 6:3 (December 1987), 306–326.

Murphy, J. E., *The Random Character of Interest Rates,* Probus Publishing Company, Chicago, Illinois, 1990.

The implications of randomness for bond investment are given in Murphy, J. E., *With Interest: How to Profit From Interest Rate Fluctuations,* Dow-Jones Irwin, Homewood, IL, 1986.

Chapter 27—Five Laws of Finance

The first law follows from a natural property of the random walk. If the steps (the first differences in the logs) are independent, or nearly independent, i.e., small or zero correlation, the successive positions themselves (the sum of the steps) are highly correlated (second law). See Osborne, M.F.M., *The Stock Market and Finance from a Physicist's Viewpoint,* published by the author (1977), 11104 Hollybroche Court, Oakta, VA, 22124, Vol. II., 477.

Murphy, J.E. and Nelson, J.R., "A Note on the Stability of P/E Ratios," *Financial Analysts Journal* (March-April 1969), 77–80.

Murphy, J.E. and Nelson, J.R., "Random and Nonrandom Relationships Among Financial Variables: A Financial Model," *Journal of Financial and Quantitative Analysis,* VI:2 (March 1971), 875–885.

Murphy, J.E. and Nelson, J.R., "Five Principles of Financial Relationships," *Financial Analysts Journal,* 27:2 (March-April 1971), 38–52.

Murphy, J.E., "Five New Financial Principles: Reply to a Comment," *Financial Analysts Journal,* 28:2 (March-April 1972), 112.

APPENDIX X

Bibliography

One of the best articles on the stock market is Osborne's "Brownian Motion in the Stock Market." Though technical, it lays out the underlying character of the market and shows the effect of the holding period (time) on dispersion. Osborne's article, and a number of others, may be found in Cootner's *The Random Character of the Stock Market.* Richard Brealey's *An Introduction to Risk and Return from Common Stocks* and *Security Prices in a Competitive Market* provide good overviews of the subject and, unlike Cootner, are not technical.

Probably the best treatment of randomness in earnings is Rayner and Little's *Higgledy, Piggledy Growth Again,* though it deals with British data. The other principal articles—there aren't very many—are listed in the bibliography. Apart from the studies of Russell Nelson and me, there is little work on randomness in other financial variables. Both subjects deserve more study, preferably along the lines of Osborne's "Brownian Motion." Brealey covers randomness in earnings.

I am not aware that others have classified variables or drawn inferences from that classification in the way done here.

One of the best studies of the cross-sectional behavior of stock prices is Fisher and Lorie's "Some Studies of Variability of Returns on Investments in Common Stocks" which appeared in the *Journal of Business* in 1970. Although the article is entirely descriptive, an excellent theoretical analysis and summary was given by Latane in a 1973 issue of the same journal; it is called "Cross-Section Regularities on Returns on Investments in Common Stocks.

There are many studies on the return on the market over time, nearly all descriptive, few analytic.

There are even more studies on reducing portfolio risk, most of them theoretical, some descriptive, mainly on the beta controversy. Markowitz's *Portfolio Selection* is a classic and is probably the best. It is standard statistics, except for the discussion of the "efficient frontier." That concept is difficult to apply because the inputs are unknowable, though this weakness does not seem to have diminished the popularity of the topic.

Many valuable empirical analyses of credit problems have been done, usually under the topic of predicting bankruptcy. Prominent is the work of Altman and Beaver. Nearly all of this work has an unnecessary weakness: the variables from which the predictive formulas are derived are not dimensionless, though they could be. Altman, for example, uses sales in calculating his equations. The use of sales makes the result particular and arbitrary. It would have been preferable to divide variables by their standard deviation and thereby achieve a generality that crossed industry lines and permits application of probability theory to the issue. The result would be a different and, I think, more useful perspective.

The prediction of loss in this book—the same underlying problem as bankruptcy—uses a dimensionless variable; this permits putting the analysis in terms of probability and deriving an analytical tool that is independent of industry. See Murphy and Osborne, "Predicting the Probability of Loss." The probability chapters in this book illustrate how that can be done. The other literature on this approach is limited.

The other references that I found particularly useful are mentioned in the text. In general, the work that was most helpful to me came not from students of finance, but from outsiders like Feller, Mandelbrot (*Fractals*) and Osborne who looked at the data from a slightly different perspective, who viewed it in more general terms, and tried to apply probability to the subject matter.

Aitchison, J. and Brown, J.A.C., *The Lognormal Distribution with Special Reference to its Uses in Economics*, Cambridge University Press, London, 1981.

Alexander, G. and Francis, J.C., *Portfolio Analysis*, Prentice-Hall, New York, 1986.

Ambrose, Brent W., Ancel, Esther W., and Griffiths, Mark D., "Fractal Structure in the Capital Markets Revisited," *Financial Analysts Journal* 49 (June 1993), 73–77.

Barnes, A. and Downes, D., "A Reexamination of the Empirical Distribution of Stock Price Changes," *Journal of the American Statistical Association*, 68 (June 1973), 348–350.

Beaver, William H., "Financial Ratios as Predictions of Failure," *Empirical Research in Accounting: Selected Studies, 1966*, Supplement to Vol. 4, *Journal of Accounting Research*, 62–87.

Beaver, William H., "The Time Series Behavior of Earnings," *Empirical Research in Accounting: Selected Studies, 1970*, Supplement to Vol. 8, *Journal of Accounting Research*, 62–87.

Black, F. and Scholes, M., "The Effects of Dividend Yield and Dividend Policy on Common Stock Prices and Returns," *Journal of Financial Economics*, 1 (May 1974), 1–22.

Blattberg, Robert C. and Gonedes, Nicholas J., "A Comparison of the Stable and Student Distributions as Statistical Models for Stock Prices," *Journal of Business*, 47 (April 1974), 244–280.

Blattberg, Robert C. and Gonedes, Nicholas J., "A Comparison of the Stable and Student Distributions as Statistical Models for Stock Prices: Reply," *Journal of Business*, 50 (January 1977), 78–79.

Blume, Marshall E., "On the Assessment of Risk," *Journal of Finance*, 27 (March 1971), 1–10.

Boness, A.A. Chen and Jatusipitak, S., "Investigation of Nonstationarity in Prices," *Journal of Business*, 47 (October 1974), 518–537.

Brealey, Richard A., *An Introduction to Risk and Return from Common Stocks*, Cambridge, M.I.T. Press, 1969.

Brealey, Richard A., *Security Prices in a Competitive Market*, Cambridge, M.I.T. Press, 1971.

Brealey, Richard A., "The Distribution and Independence of Successive Rates of Return in the U.S. Equity Markets," *Journal of Business Finance*, 43 (Summer 1970), 29–40.

Brennan, Michael J., "The Optimal Number of Securities in a Risky Asset Portfolio When There are Fixed Costs of Transactions: Theory and Some Empirical Results," *Journal of Financial and Quantitative Analysis*, 10 (September 1975), 483–496.

Brigham, Eugene F. and Pappas, James L., "Duration of Growth, Changes in Growth Rates, and Corporate Share Prices," *Financial Analysts Journal*, 22 (May–June 1966), 157–161.

Brigham, Eugene F. and Pappas, James L., "Rates of Return on Common Stocks," *Journal of Business*, 41 (July 1969), 302–330.

Brooks, Leroy D. and Buckmaster, D.A., "Further Evidence of the Time Series Properties of Accounting Income," *Journal of Finance*, 31 (December 1975), 1359–1372.

Campanella, F.B., *The Measurement of Portfolio Risk Exposure*, Lexington Books, Lexington, Mass, 1972.

Cohn, Timothy A., "Adjusted Maximum Likelihood Estimation of the Moments of Log-normal Populations from Type I Censored Samples," U.S. Geological Survey, Reston, Va., 1987.

Cooley, Philip L., Roenfeldt, Rodney L., and Modanni, Naval K., "Interdependence of Market Risk Measures," *Journal of Business* 50 (July 1977), 356–363.

Cootner, P.H., Ed., *The Random Character of Stock Prices*, Cambridge, M.I.T. Press, 1964.

Elton, Edwin J. and Gruber, Martin, J., "Risk Reduction and Portfolio Size: An Analytical Solution," *Journal of Business*, 50 (October 1977), 415–437.

Evans, John L. and Archer, Stephen H., "Diversification and the Reduction of Dispersion: An Empirical Analysis," *Journal of Finance* 23 (December 1966), 761–767.

Fama, E.F., "Random Walks in Stock Market Prices," *Financial Analysts Journal*, 21 (September–October 1965), 55–58.

Fama, Eugene F., "The Behavior of Stock Market Prices," *Journal of Business*, 38 (January 1965), 45–46.

Feder, Jens, *Fractals*, Plenum Press, New York, 1988.

Feller, W., *An Introduction to Probability Theory and its Applications*, Vol. I, 2nd ed., Wiley, New York, 1957, 344.

Feller, W., "The Asymptomatic Distribution of the Range of Sums of Random Variables," *Annals of Mathematical Statistics*, 22 (1951), 427–432.

Fisher, L., "Outcomes for 'Random' Investment in Common Stocks Listed on the New York Stock Exchange," *Journal of Business*, 38 (April 1965), 149–161.

Fisher, Lawrence, and Lorie, James H., *A Half Century of Returns on Stocks and Bonds*, University of Chicago, 1977.

Fisher, Lawrence, and Lorie, James H., "Some Studies of Variability of Returns on Investments in Common Stocks," *Journal of Business*, 43 (April 1970), 99–134.

Flavin, Marjorie A., "Excess Volatility in the Financial Markets: A Reassessment of the Empirical Evidence," *Journal of Political Economy*, 91 (December 1983), 929–956.

Fleming, Robert M., "How Risky is the Market," *Journal of Business*, 46 (July 1973), 404–424.

Friend, Irwin and Vickers, Douglas, "Portfolio Selection and Investment Performance," *Journal of Finance*, 20 (September 1965), 391–415.

Fogler, H. Russell, *Analyzing the Stock Market: A Quantitative Approach*, Grid, Inc., Columbus, Ohio, 1973.

Garman, M.B. and Klass, M.J., "On the Estimation of Security Price Volatilities from Historical Data," *Journal of Business*, 53 (January 1980), 67–78.

Guerard, John and Vaught, H.T., *The Handbook of Financial Modeling*, Probus Publishing Company, Chicago, 1989.

Ibbotson, Roger G. and Sinquefield, Rex A., "Stocks, Bonds, Bills, and Inflation: Year-by-Year Historical Returns (1926-1974)," *Journal of Business*, 49 (January 1976), 11–47.

Ibbotson & Associates, *Stocks, Bonds, Bills, & Inflation, 1991 Yearbook*, Chicago, 1991, Exhibit C-2.

Ibbotson, R.G. and Brinson, G.P., *Investment Markets*, McGraw-Hill, New York, 1986.

Jennings, Edward, "An Empirical Analysis of Some Aspects of Common Stock Diversification," *Journal of Financial and Quantitative Analysis*, 6 (March 1971), 797–813.

Johnson, A. and Shannon, B., "A Note on the Diversification and Reduction of Risk," *Journal of Financial Economics*, 1 (1974), 365–372.

King, Benjamin F., "Market and Industry Factors in Stock Price Behavior," *Journal of Business*, 39 (January 1966), 139–190.

Kolb, Robert W., *Options: The Investor's Complete Toolkit*, New York Institute of Finance, New York, 1991.

Latane, Henry A., "Cross-Section Regularities in Returns on Investments in Common Stocks," *Journal of Business*, 46 (October 1973), 512–517.

Lewis, Alan L., Kassdout, Sheen T., Brehm, Dennis R., and Johnston, Jack, "The Ibbotson-Sinquefield Simulation Made Easy," *The Journal of Business*, 53 (April 1980), 205–214.

Lintner, John, "Security Prices, Risk, and Maximal Gains from Diversification," *Journal of Finance*, December 1965.

Lintner, John, "Distribution of Incomes of Corporations Among Dividends, Retained Earnings and Taxes," *American Economic Review*, 46 (May 1956), 97–113.

Lintner, John and Glauber, Robert, "Higgledy Piggledy Growth in America?" Seminar on the Analysis of Security Prices, Center for Research in Security Prices, Graduate School of Business, The University of Chicago, May 11–12, 1967.

Lorie, James H. and Hamilton, Mary T., *The Stock Market: Theories and Evidence*, Richard D. Irwin, Homewood, Ill., 1973.

Lorie, James, H., "Some Comments on Recent Quantitative and Formal Research on the Stock Market," *Journal of Business*, 39 (January 1966), 107–109.

Maginn, John L. and Tuttle, Donald L., editors, *Managing Investment Portfolios: A Dynamic Process*, Warren, Gorham & Lamont, Boston, 1983.

Mains, Norman E., "Risk, the Pricing of Capital Assets, and the Evaluation of Investment Portfolios: Comment," *Journal of Business* 50 (July 1977), 371–384.

Mandelbrot, B., *Fractals*, W.H. Freeman, San Francisco, 1977.

Mandelbrot, B., "The Variation of Certain Speculative Prices," *Journal of Business*, 36 (October 1963), 394–419.

Mandelbrot, Benoit, "Forecasts of Future Prices, Unbiased Markets, and 'Martingale' Models," *Journal of Business*, 39 (January 1966), 242–255.

Mandelbrot, B. and Fama, E.F., "The Behavior of Stock Market Prices," *Journal of Business*, 38 (January 1965), 34–105.

Mandelbrot, B. and Taylor, H.M., "On the Distribution of Stock Price Differences," *Operations Research*, 15 (1967), 1057–1062.

Markowitz, Harry, *Portfolio Selection*, New York, Wiley, 1959.

Markowitz, Harry, "Markowitz Revisited," *Financial Analysts Journal*, 32 (September–October 1976), 47–52.

McEnally, R.W. and Todd, R.B., "Cross-Sectional Variation in Common Stock Returns, *Financial Analysts Journal*, 48 (May–June 1992), 77–78, Table I.

Miller, M. and Modigliani, F., "Dividend Policy, Growth, and the Valuation of Shares," *Journal of Business*, (October 1961), 411–433.

Murphy, J.E., *The Random Character of Interest Rates*, Probus Publishing Company, Chicago, 1990.

Murphy, J.E., *With Interest: How to Profit From Fluctuations in Interest Rates*, Dow Jones-Irwin, Homewood, Ill., 1987.

Murphy, J.E., "Relative Growth of Earnings. Per Share—Past and Future," *Financial Analysts Journal*, 22 (November–December 1966), 73–76.

Murphy, J.E., "Return on Equity Capital, Dividend Payout and Growth of Earnings Per Share," *Financial Analysts Journal*, 23 (May–June 1967), 91–93.

Murphy, J.E., "Earnings Growth and Price Change in the Same Time Period," *Financial Analysts Journal*, 24 (January–February 1968), 97–99.

Murphy, J.E., "Effect of Leverage on Profitability, Growth and Market Valuation of Common Stock," *Financial Analysts Journal*, 24 (July–August 1968), 121–123.

Murphy, J.E. and Johnson, R.S., "Predicting Dividend Changes," *Trusts & Estates*, (August 1972), 638–641.

Murphy, J.E. and Nelson, J.R., "A Note on the Stability of P/E Ratios," *Financial Analysts Journal*, 25 (March–April 1969), 77–80.

Murphy, J.E., and Nelson, J.R., "Random and Nonrandom Relationships Among Financial Variables: A Financial Model," *Journal of Financial and Quantitative Analysis*, VI:2 (March 1971), 875–885.

Murphy, J.E. and Nelson, J.R., "Five Principles of Financial Relationships," *Financial Analysts Journal*, 27:2 (March–April 1971), 38–52. Reprinted in The Institute of Chartered Financial Analysts, *SUPPLEMENTARY READINGS IN FINANCIAL ANALYSIS: 1972*, 1971. R.D. Irwin, Homewood, Ill., 208–222.

Murphy, J.E. and Nelson, J.R., "Five New Financial Principles: Reply to a Comment," *Financial Analysts Journal*, 28 (March–April 1972), 112.

Murphy, J.E. and Osborne, M.F.M., "Games of Chance and the Probability of Corporate Profit or Loss," *Financial Management*, 8:2 (Summer 1979), 82–88.

Murphy, J.E. and Osborne, M.F.M., "Predicting the Volatility of Interest Rates," *Journal of Portfolio Management*, (Winter (1985), 66–69.

Murphy, J.E. and Osborne, M.F.M., "Brownian Motion in the Bond Market," *The Review of Futures Markets*, 6:3 (December 1987), 306–326.

Murphy, J.E. and Stevenson, H.W., "Price/Earnings Ratios and Future Growth of Earnings and Dividends," *Financial Analysts Journal*, 23:6 (November–December 1967), 111–114.

Nicholson, S.F., "Price—Earnings Ratios," *Financial Analysts Journal*, 16 (July–August 1960), 43–46.

Niederhoffer, Victor and Regan, P.J., "Earnings Changes, Analysts' Forecasts and Stock Prices," *Financial Analysts Journal*, 28 (May–June 1972), 65–71.

Officer, R.R., "The Variability of the Market Factor of the New York Stock Exchange," *Journal of Business*, 46 (July 1973), 434–453.

Officer, R.R., "The Distribution of Stock Returns," *The Journal of the American Statistical Association*, 67 (December 1972), 807–812.

Osborne, M.F.M., "Brownian Motion in the Stock Market," *Operations Research*, 7 (1959), 145–173. Also in Cootner.

Osborne, M.F.M., *The Stock Market and Finance from a Physicist's Viewpoint*, published by the author (1977), 11104 Hollybrooke Court, Oakton, Va., 22124.

Osborne, M.F.M. and Murphy, J.E., "Brownian Motion of Corporate Earnings in a Varying Probability Field," Fall 1980 Seminar, Institute for Quantitative Research in Finance. Available from the Institute, Columbia University, New York, N.Y.

Osborne, M.F.M. and Murphy, J.E., "Financial Analogs of Physical Brownian Motion, as Illustrated by Earnings," *The Financial Review*, 19:2 (1984), 153–172.

Osborne, M.F.M. and Murphy, J.E., "Brownian Motion in the Interest Rate Considered as the Price of Money," Eastern Finance Association, Annual Meeting, April 20–23, 1983, New York, N.Y.

Parkinson, Michael, "The Extreme Value Method for Estimating the Variance of the Rate of Return," *Journal of Business*, 53 (January 1980), 61–66.

Peters, Edgar E., *Chaos and Order in the Capital Markets: A New View of Cycles, Prices, and Market Volatility*, John Wiley & Sons, Inc., New York, 1991.

Peters, Edgar E., "Fractal Structure in the Capital Markets," *Financial Analysts Journal*, 45 (July/August 1989), 32–37.

Peters, Edgar E., "R/S Analysis Using Logarithmic Returns," *Financial Analysts Journal*, 48 (November/December 1992), 81–82.

Price, Lee N., "Choosing Between Growth and Yield," *Financial Analysts Journal*, 35 (July–August 1979).

Praetz, Peter D., "The Distribution of Share Price Changes," *Journal of Business*, 45 (January 1972), 49–55.

Praetz, Peter D., "A Comparison of the Stable and Student Distributions as Statistical Models for Stock Prices: Comment," *Journal of Business*, 50 (January 1977), 76–77.

Rayner, A.C. and Little, I.M.D., *Higgledy Piggledy Growth Again*, Basil Blackwell, Oxford, 1966.

Rothstein, Marvin, "On Geometric and Arithmetic Portfolio Performance Indexes," *Journal of Financial and Quantitative Analysis*, 7 (September 1972), 1983–1992.

Ross, Stephen A., "Is Beta Useful?" *The CAPM Controversy*, AIMR, Charlottesville, Va., 1993.

Salomon Brothers, *Analytical Record of Yields and Yield Spreads from 1945*, New York, January 1993.

Schwert, G. William, "Indexes of U.S. Stock Prices from 1802 to 1987," *Journal of Business*, 63 (1990), 399–426.

Sharpe, William F., "Risk Aversion in the Stock Market: Some Empirical Evidence," *Journal of Finance*, 20 (September 1965), 416–422.

Sharpe, William F., "Mutual Fund Performance," *Journal of Business*, 39 (January 1966), 119–138.

Sharpe, William F., *Investments*, 3rd. ed., Prentice Hall, New York, 1985.

Scott, M.F.G., "Relative Share Prices and Yields," *Oxford Economic Papers*, (October 1962), 218–250.

Teichmoeller, J., "Distribution of Stock Price Changes," *Journal of the American Statistical Association*, 66 (June 1971), 282–284.

Wagner, W. and Lau, S., "The Effect of Diversification on Risk," *Financial Analysts Journal*, 27 (November–December 1971), 48–53.

Whitmore, G.A., "Diversification and the Reduction of Dispersion: A Note," *Journal of Financial and Quantitative Analysis*, 5 (June 1970), 263–264.

Young, W.E. and Trent, R.H., "Geometric Mean Approximations of Individual Security and Portfolio Performance," *Journal of Financial and Quantitative Analysis*, 4 (June 1969), 179–200.

Index